SOUTHAMPTON

A POTTED HISTORY

MARTIN BRISLAND

AMBERLEY

This book is dedicated to the memory of my fellow tour guide Steve Roberts (1965–2022)

First published 2023

Amberley Publishing
The Hill, Stroud
Gloucestershire, GL5 4EP

www.amberley-books.com

Copyright © Martin Brisland, 2023

The right of Martin Brisland to be identified as the
Author of this work has been asserted in accordance
with the Copyrights, Designs and Patents Act 1988.

ISBN 978 1 3981 0818 9 (print)
ISBN 978 1 3981 0819 6 (ebook)

British Library Cataloguing in Publication Data.
A catalogue record for this book is available from the
British Library.

Typesetting by SJmagic DESIGN SERVICES, India.
Printed in Great Britain.

Contents

Introduction

This is my fifth book for Amberley Publishing, following on from *Secret Southampton, A–Z of Southampton, Secret New Forest* and *Celebrating Southampton*. Having recovered from a brain haemorrhage in 2017, it is a milestone I am very grateful to have achieved. By definition a potted history is a selective overview of Southampton's stories. There are many comprehensive histories of Southampton for further reading. I hope you will find this book informative, educational and interesting. I would also like to thank Julian Porter for his excellent photography and support.

Overview

A Roman settlement, the UK's third longest medieval fortifications stretching 2 km, Henry V's troops departing to eventually fight the French at Agincourt in 1415, provisioning the *Mayflower* in 1620 for its journey to America, a Georgian spa town, local crew perishing on the *Titanic*, becoming 'Gateway to the World', the iconic Spitfire, the Second World War bombing, D-Day departures and today the cruise capital of Europe – Southampton's seen it all.

Influenced by Saxon, Viking, Norman and European traders and invaders, Southampton flourished, becoming a huge exporter of wool and a major early importer of wine, with many underground vaults to prove it.

INTERESTING EXTRA
The vaults can still be visited today on a See Southampton guided tour. They proved particularly useful during the Second World War when some served as underground air-raid shelters.

Southampton's reputation as a leading trading centre was such that in 1338 a combined fleet of fifty French, Genoese and Monégasque swept through Southampton on a murderous looting rampage. It prompted Edward III, whose wine cellar had been ransacked, to order further fortification of the walls.

Head of the Monégasque, Charles Grimaldi, used his share of the Southampton booty to found Monaco.

During the 1750–1830 spa town period, the Georgians flocked to the city, bathed in its waters, built fine mansions and held grand parties in the Assembly Rooms.

The first meeting of the Southampton Dock Company was in August 1836 and with the arrival of the railway from London in May 1840, Southampton's shipping industry blossomed. By 1907 it was Britain's premier passenger port.

The White Star Dock, later known as Ocean Dock, opened in 1911. It was from here that the *Titanic* left Southampton on 10 April 1912. The Titanic disaster was deeply felt in Southampton, where over 500 households lost a family member.

In the 1930s, ships sailed from Southampton across the Atlantic and around the globe, making it the 'Gateway to the World'.

The area around Southampton Docks was heavily bombed in the Second World War. The Supermarine Spitfire fighter plane was developed on the bank of the River Itchen at Woolston and was also bombed. Since the Second World War, Southampton has been rebuilt.

By the 1970s sea travel had declined as air travel became the norm. Some of the old docks were converted into areas of shops, offices and marinas. Today, it has become the cruise capital of Europe. Many ships include Southampton on their maiden voyage as a prestigious port of call.

Before the Romans Arrived

Many finds from pre-Roman times have been found in and around Southampton.

Old Stone Age (2.5 million–10000 BC)

Animal bones were dredged up when Southampton Eastern Docks were being built from the late 1830s onwards. Also in the nineteenth century, tools and flint axes dating to over 70,000 years ago were found at gravel pits and quarry sites, particularly in the Highfield area.

Middle Stone Age (10000–4000 BC)

A flint-working site was discovered in the 1990s at Priory Avenue in St Denys. In 1999, the submerged remains of an ancient forest and cliffs were discovered off the coast at Bouldnor on the Isle of Wight. Around 8,000 years ago the Island would have been connected to the mainland. Worked timbers suggest there was boat building. Wheat was found to be non-native to the UK, suggesting trading with Europe.

In 1991, the Maritime Archaeological Trust was established in Southampton and still dives on the site every year.

New Stone Age (4000 BC–2000 BC)

At this time humans went from hunter-gatherers to farmers. Monuments such as long barrows and henges were built, such as Stonehenge. Neolithic pottery has been found near Hill Lane in Shirley, at Nursling Plantation, Lower Brownhill Road, and Chilworth Common. The Southampton area has had human settlements since the late New Stone Age. We are in a unique location with a sheltered microclimate, local rivers for transport and a double tide in Southampton Water. On Southampton Common objects were found by gravediggers working in the Old Cemetery and during the construction of the Victorian reservoirs.

The Sea City and Tudor House museums have excellent collections of finds, including a flint palaeolithic era hand axe. The Southampton Historic Environment Record (HER) database records all archaeological fieldwork that has taken place in the city.

Bronze Age (3300–750 BC)

In the nineteenth century, gravediggers at the cemetery on Southampton Common, and workmen at the site of the reservoir, sold the bronze artefacts they found to local antiquarians.

At Testwood Lakes there is part of the earliest bridge ever identified in Britain, dated to around 1500 BC. It was up to 22 metres long and found by Southern Water in 1988.

Two parallel rows of timbers were found crossing an old river course. The bridge was about 26 metres long and between 1.5 metres and 2 metres wide. A radiocarbon test dated

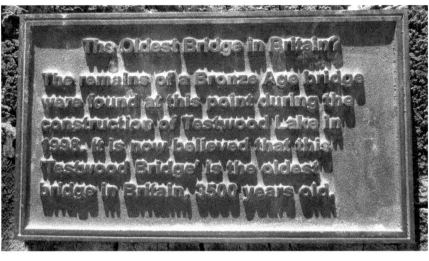

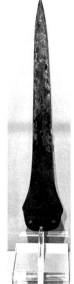

Above: The oldest bridge in Britain?

Right: Bronze Age rapier blade.

the wood to around 1,500 BC, the oldest definitely established bridge in England. People had used bronze tools to fashion the wood and a rapier blade is now displayed in Eling Tide Mill Museum.

Iron Age (750 BC–AD 43)

Earthworks have been found at Lordswood and Aldermoor. A possible salt production site was excavated at the Southampton Institute, now Solent University, and pottery has been found at Regents Park. Traces of Iron Age buildings, together with artefacts, have been found during excavations at York Buildings and Maddison Street off Upper Bugle Street.

Roman Southampton

The Belgae tribe were dominant in the area until the Roman conquest of southern England. It started in AD 43 under Emperor Claudius, lasting until AD 84 after the defeat of Boudica's army in AD 61.

The Antonine Itinerary VII, a register of Roman stations, documents the Roman settlement of Clausentum, built around AD 70. The Roman name of Clausentum is Latin in origin, from the verb *claudo* meaning an enclosed place.

It was probably at Bitterne Manor, a spit of land projecting into the River Itchen. Across it is a fortification consisting of a ditch, earthwork and wall. The outer defensive wall from around 280 was 9 feet thick with an earthen mound behind it and towers at its ends. The triangular enclosure was about 51 acres. Archaeological excavations at Clausentum were conducted in 1935 and 1951. They found remains of a road which was thought to run to Wickham. Other finds included an altar dedicated to the Celtic local river goddess Ancasta. The name means 'fast going one' and is in SeaCity Museum.

Roman Road in Chilworth and Vespasian Road in Bitterne Manor are modern reminders of Roman influence.

Across the river were remains of a Roman pier. In total 179 piles, four horizontal planks and three braces were discovered. Dating of the wood suggests the pier was built before 318. Clausentum's streets were laid out in a grid pattern. The Roman armies left Britain by 407 and the town of Clausentum was abandoned soon afterward.

The Bishop of Winchester first mentions a manor house in the late eleventh century; it was a ruin by the sixteenth century. Its stone, along with that of the Roman wall, were used to build Pear Tree House and Pear Tree Church. A new manor house was built on the site in 1804. This structure was hit by a bomb during the Second World War after which the house was rebuilt and converted into flats.

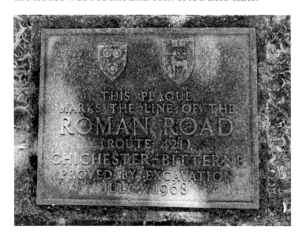

A plaque marking the site of a Roman road from Chichester to Bitterne is on Freemantle Common.

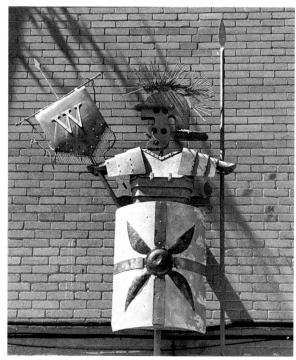

Right: Roman soldier in Thornhill.

Below: View of the site of Clausentum from across the River Itchen.

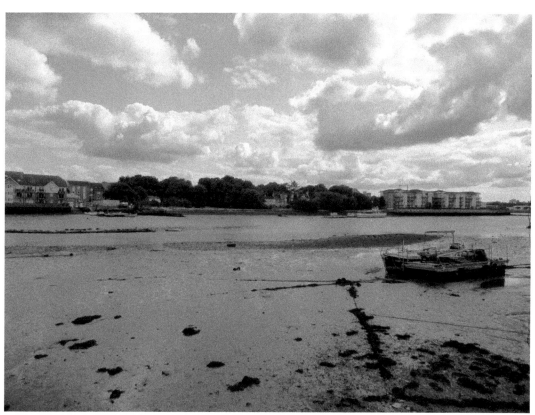

4

Anglo-Saxon Southampton
(c. 500–1066)

According to the Venerable Bede (672–735), the Jutes from northern Denmark settled in our area. By the eighth century a Saxon settlement had been established on the west bank of the Itchen, though nothing remains above ground.

It was listed in the Burghal Hidage, an early tenth-century document detailing a list of burhs (fortified towns) in the Kingdom of Wessex. It was valued at 150 hides, small when compared to Chichester, which was measured at 1,500 hides.

Th Anglo-Saxons moved their settlement across the River Itchen from the Roman settlement at Bitterne Manor to what is now the St Mary's area. It was known as Hamwic or Hamtun – the two names co-existed and described the same area. Hamtun was known as a trading town or a 'wic', which led to it being referred to as Hamwic.

One of the earliest references to Hamwic is from the Life of St. Willibald. In AD 721 the saint is recorded as boarding a vessel to be taken across the channel into France on his way to Rome. By the middle of the eleventh century, the area was described as South Hamtun by the Anglo-Saxon Chroniclers.

Slaves bound for the markets at Rouen, hunting dogs, wool, cloth, and hides have all been recorded as being exported out of Hamwic.

In AD 764 a destructive fire was recorded as having affected parts of Hamwic. Around this time, Hamwic had gained enough importance to have given its name to the shire of Hampshire. As Hamwic was also known as Hamtun, the shire was actually called Hamtunscire, hence Hampshire.

Work by Addyman and Hill between 1968 and 1971 and the 1980s resulted in heightened interest in Hamwic's past. In 1988, they claimed that the archaeological evidence suggests that the site of the town was 111 acres.

It had planned, gravelled streets and plots of land for housing and industrial use. The main north–south running street is today known as St Mary's Street. Through the discovery of post holes, there is evidence for over sixty Anglo-Saxon era buildings of various uses within Hamwic.

Quern-stones used to grind seeds into grain have been found. We now know they came from the Rhineland and the Low Countries. Likewise glass and pottery shards have been traced back to their places of origin in northern France, Scandinavia, the Rhineland and the Low Countries.

The discovery of a richly furnished burial dating to the seventeenth century indicates there was a wealthy elite around the town.

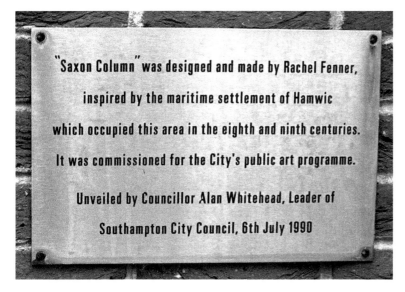

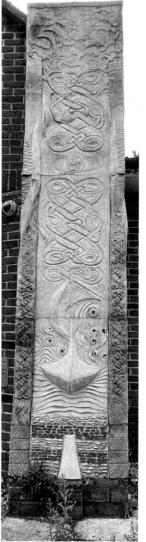

"Saxon Column" was designed and made by Rachel Fenner, inspired by the maritime settlement of Hamwic which occupied this area in the eighth and ninth centuries. It was commissioned for the City's public art programme.

Unveiled by Councillor Alan Whitehead, Leader of Southampton City Council, 6th July 1990

Above: Saxon Column plaque.

Right: The Saxon Column in St Mary's Street.

The royal mint of Hamwic was used by the kings of Wessex between AD 786 and 858. King Ine devoted not only to Christianity but to the political and economic functioning of Wessex may have founded the mint. Over 200 sceatta have been found.

Excavations were undertaken in the late 1990s prior to the building of the new St Mary's Football Stadium. As well as an early Saxon cemetery, traces of a street and of wattle and daub buildings were found, including the possible site of a blacksmith's workshop. Under St Mary's Stadium forty burial graves were found dating back to the seventh century. Along with human remains, objects were found that were meant to help them in the afterlife, indicating that the early inhabitants of Hamwic were not Christian.

The settlement stretched as far as Six Dials to the north and to Hoglands in the west. It is estimated that at its peak up to 4,000 people lived in Hamwic.

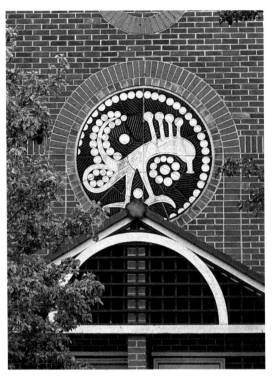 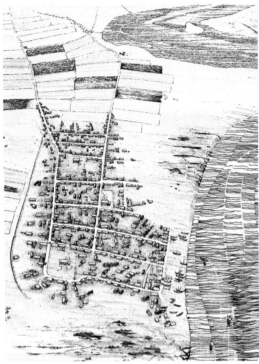

Above left: Design on Nos 61–67 Brinton Road, St Mary's, based on coins minted during Saxon times.

Above right: Impression of Hamwic AD 750. A Saxon town on the west bank of the River Itchen.

When St Mary's Football Stadium opened in 2001 manager Gordon Strachan had a lengthy winless run. He contacted a pagan white witch, Cerridwen Dragon Oak Connelly. The ceremony she performed on the pitch did the trick, with Southampton winning their next home game.

In 840 the Aeldorman of Wessex, Wulfheard, defeated a fleet of Danish ships near Hamwic. Two years later the Vikings were back and this time they succeeded in ravaging the town.

In the reign of Alfred the Great (848–899), Winchester was fortified and many inhabitants of Hamwic moved behind its safe walls and the town began to decline.

Another town was established to the south-west with its own protective enclosure. By the tenth century this new town of South Hamtun was operational.

The Battle of Edington took place in May 878 about 40 miles north of Southampton. King Alfred the Great, with his army from Wessex, defeated the Vikings led by the Dane Guthrum. It resulted in maintaining Anglo-Saxon independence from the Danes, who had conquered East Anglia, Mercia and Northumbria. Even though the original Anglo-Saxon trading town of Hamwic did not survive past the tenth century, its successor Southampton has carried on its spirit through to the present day.

5

Vikings
(789–1066)

The first recorded raid on England was in AD 789 at Portland in Dorset. They exploited divisions in the Anglo-Saxon kingdoms to overwhelm them until Wessex under King Alfred was the last kingdom standing.

In AD 994 a combined force of the Danish king Sweyn Forkbeard and the Norwegian Olaf Tryggvarson wintered in Southampton.

For a while in the early eleventh century, England became part of a Scandinavian empire under King Cnut. After Cnut there was a short Saxon restoration under Edward the Confessor. The Battle of Hastings in 1066 ushered in the era of Norman rule.

The Danish King Cnut was declared king in 1016 on Southampton Common by the Witan, the council of the Anglo-Saxon kings. He was crowned King of England in Winchester after defeating the Anglo-Saxon King Aethelred the Unready.

While in Southampton Cnut is reputed to have sat in his chair on the seashore and said to the rising tide, 'I command you not to rise on to my land, nor to presume to wet my clothing or limbs.' It is thought that this was not an act of arrogance but to demonstrate that he was only human. The sea-soaked king declared that there is no king worthy of the name save God.

Did his attempt to hold back the tide happen here in 1028? No one can say for sure and Bosham in West Sussex also claims the story.

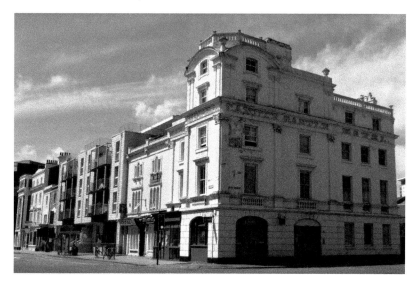

The Canute Castle
Hotel, Canute Road.

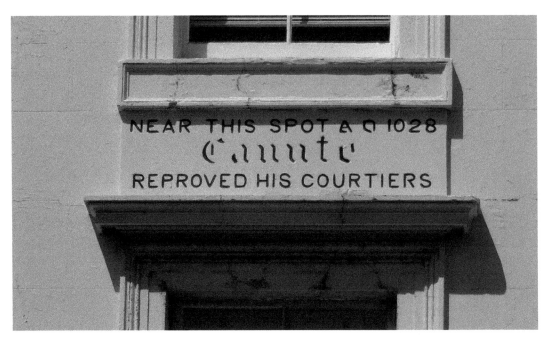

NEAR THIS SPOT A D 1028
Canute
REPROVED HIS COURTIERS

Did Canute reprove his courtiers here in 1028?

We do have local references to Cnut including Canute Road, the former Canute Hotel and Canute Chambers, once the offices of the White Star Line. There is also the misnamed Canute's Palace which in fact is a Norman merchant's house built around 100 years after the reign of Canute. In 1968 the docks acquired a 200-ton floating crane called Canute.

Olaf's Tun in Woolston has been a craft ale bar since 2016. This was possibly the original name for Woolston when the Vikings had a small fort or 'tun' here. In AD 994 they named themselves after their leader King Olaf I of Norway, hence Olaf's Tun, a name that is mentioned in the Domesday Book of 1086. The alternative spellings Oluvestune/Olvestune/Wulf's Tun can also be found.

INTERESTING EXTRA
Until the Southampton Ice Rink closed in 1988, the ice hockey team was known as Southampton Vikings.

1066 and All That

In 1066 William the Conqueror defeated the last Saxon king, Harold, at the Battle of Hastings to bring in the era of Norman rule. During the Norman period, Southampton became a major port connecting Winchester with Normandy.

A castle was built not long after 1066. The Castle Way flats are on the site today in the north-western part of the Old Town. It was first mentioned in 1154 and again in 1378 during improvements after the French raid. Two garderobes, probably installed around 1250, used tidal sea water to create a type of flush toilet system for the castle. The castle had a beacon on top as part of a warning system. Parts survive such as the castle bailey wall near the Forty Steps, the main hall and a large barrel vault where the king's wine was stored.

Not maintained as a royal castle, it fell into disrepair and was sold off in 1618. Much of its stone was used by locals and for repairs to the walls. There was a later mock-Gothic folly castle, built by the 3rd Marquess of Lansdowne, that lasted for a few years in the very early 1800s.

The town was governed by the mayor, sheriff, town sargeant and the burgesses, all Norman merchants.

The Normans were building St Michael's Church by 1070, St Michael being the patron saint of Normandy. The church has the French cockerel on top of the spire.

The Domesday Book records that Southampton in 1086 was split into English and French quarters, the French occupying the area to the west where French Street is today. The High Street was once named English Street.

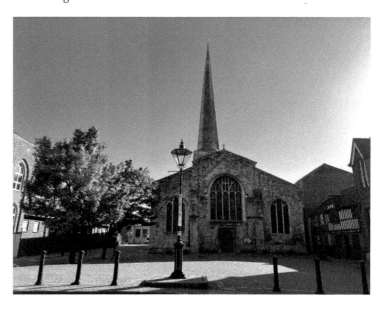

St Michael's Church.

In 1233 Walter Le Fleming granted land to a religious order. A Franciscan friary was built near God's House. From 1290 the friars pumped water from Colewell Spring in Hill Lane through lead pipes to watering points called conduits and thence to the friary. In 1311 the friars granted the use of their water to the town's inhabitants, and in 1420 they passed the whole water supply system over to the town council. This is one of the earliest examples of a municipally owned water supply in Britain. Conduit Head off Rollesbrook Greenway in Hill Lane and Conduit House opposite the Mayflower Theatre still survive.

As noted by Elsie Sandell in *Southampton Cavalcade*, during Norman and Angevin times, few towns can have had more constant associations with royalty than Southampton. William the Conqueror's son Rufus was killed in the nearby New Forest in a 'hunting incident' in 1100. This enabled William's younger son to come to the throne as Henry I. He founded the Augustinian Priory of St Denys, the foundation charter granting 'a parcel of land between Portswood and the Itchen, having a rental of 11s 6d, together with another parcel of land near the sea to the east of the borough, having a rental of 41s 6d'.

William's great-grandson Henry II married Eleanor of Aquitaine in 1152. They had eight children, including the future King Richard and King John.

During Henry II's reign from 1154 to 1189, Southampton became an importer of wine, and today the Castle Vault remains Southampton's most impressive wine vault. Here, the 'King's Prise' of one wine barrel of every ten imported would be stored.

Following the murder of his childhood friend Thomas à Becket in Canterbury Cathedral in 1170, Henry II travelled to England from France in 1174, passing along the High Street wearing a sackcloth and ashes in atonement. He then followed the Pilgrims Way to Canterbury.

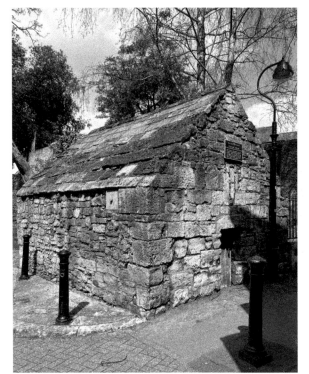

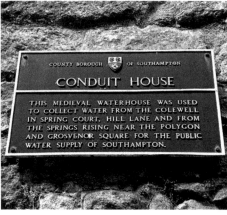

Above: Conduit House plaque.

Left: Conduit House opposite the Mayflower Theatre.

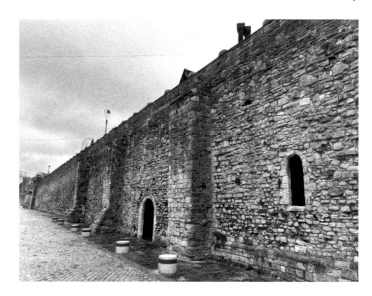

The Castle vaults entrance on the Western Wall.

King Richard I ruled from 1189 to 1199. He is often depicted as the absent king fighting in the Crusades. After his father's death, Richard sailed to the Holy Lands with an army to face Saladin. He won victories, but after failing to take Jerusalem, he reached a truce with Saladin. Travelling home through Europe he was captured in Austria, handed over to the German Emperor Henry VI, who then demanded a ransom for his release. This was raised with the help of Gervaise de Hampton, a very wealthy Southampton man. Indeed he was known as 'Gervaise Le Riche' such was his wealth!

Richard was released on 4 February 1194. There is no evidence for the story that King Richard spent his only Christmas in England at Southampton Castle in 1194, as suggested by Elsie Sandell in *Southampton Cavalcade*.

The stone building behind Tudor House is known as King John's Palace. The size of the building, and the nearby Canute's Palace, show the wealthy nature of some Southampton merchants of this period.

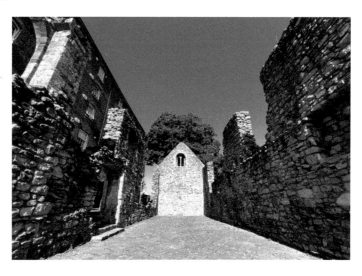

The Norman Long House in Porters Lane.

The Bargate

It is the iconic symbol of Southampton and used on the council's logo. Architectural historian Nikolaus Pevsner wrote 'The Bargate is probably the finest, and certainly the most complex, town gateway in Britain.'

The first phase was constructed around 1175 and consisted of a stone single-storey tower. Medieval carts were stopped at the Bargate to pay taxes before entering.

A second phase, which included the first floor and drum towers, was added about a hundred years later and the final stage was completed during the Hundred Years' War in the late fourteenth century.

The building has been modified and adapted over the years to reflect its changing use and the needs of the town. The ground floor of the Bargate was a prison as we know that in 1439 the bolt was repaired. The room then became the magistrates' court. In 1619 a presentment was made at the court leet for the Guildhall to be cleaned as the rushes on the floor had been there so long that they could 'breed infeccons'.

The shields above the central arch were of important local families, plus St George and St Andrew. They were removed during restoration work a few years ago to the Bargate

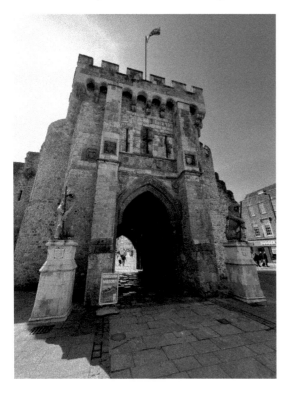

Front view of the Bargate.

stonework. Large wooden panels showing the legendary Sir Bevois and his squire Ascupart were displayed in front of the Bargate until 1881 but are now kept inside.

The earliest reference to lions at the Bargate was in 1619, when the lions were at the outer ends of the parapets to the bridge over the defensive ditch on the north side. The ditch in front was filled in by the mid-eighteenth century. There had previously been lions outside the Watergate, so they may have been moved from the southern maritime entrance to the landward entrance of Southampton.

There is a 1619 reference to revarnishing the lions to prevent them from rotting, so it is assumed they were carved from wood. New lions in 1696 were repainted in 1709 but were replaced again in 1716.The present statues probably date from 1743. The lion pedestals bear the inscription 'Richard Raymond, Esq., Mayor 1743'. Close examination of the lions suggests that they were cast by a skilled sculptor and a likely candidate is John Cheere of Hyde Park Corner, London (1709–87). They were painted a buff colour to look as if they had been carved in stone rather than clay and iron ore. They were restored to this original colour in 2021.

The Bargate has witnessed many important events. The army of Edward III passed through in 1346 on the way to the Battle of Crecy, as did Henry V's army in 1415 to fight at Agincourt. Both Charles I and II visited the Bargate and Allied soldiers marched through in the world wars.

With the introduction of the electric trams in 1900 it was suggested that the Bargate be demolished or moved to a different location such as Houndwell Park. Such suggestions about demolition were finally dismissed by the council in 1914. The last tram through the arch was in June 1938. The last one ever was on New Year's Eve 1949.

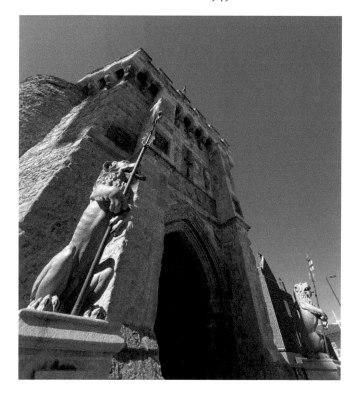

The lions restored from black to their original buff colour.

Some interesting graffiti can still be seen, dated to *c.* 1553, when the prison on the west side of the Bargate was used for minor offenders. The Bargate was used as a prison right up until Georgian times when it was relocated to God's House. The Bargate was the town's Guildhall until the 1770s. Plays were performed there in the 1590s by Lord Strange's Players from London.

On the south side of the Bargate in the niche above the archway is a statue of the body of the Roman Emperor Hadrian copied from a statue in the British Museum by Eleanor Coade. She was famous for manufacturing neoclassical figures in Lithodipyra or Coade stone. The head of this statue is in fact that of George III.

The statue was placed there in 1809 by the 3rd Marquess of Lansdowne, who wished to flatter the king by likening him to a Roman emperor. It replaced a wooden statue of Queen Anne, which was removed and placed inside the Bargate where it remains. It is minus an arm, which was damaged during VE Day celebrations in 1945. Also on the south side is the curfew bell dated 1605 and a sundial from 1705.

The recent Bargate Quarter development on the east side incorporates the remaining parts of the northern walls as a feature.

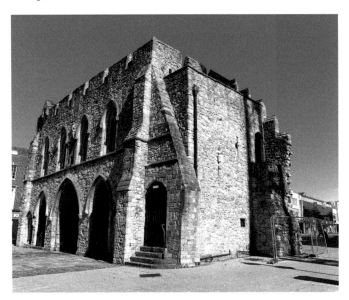

Left: South side of the Bargate.

Below: Watch bell (top left), sundial (centre) and George III statue (below).

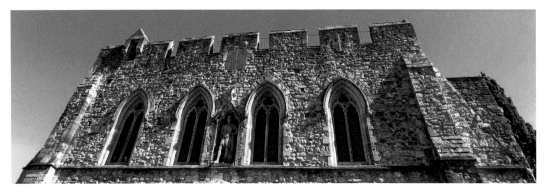

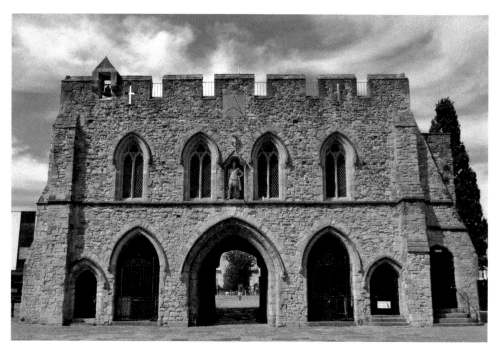

The central arch through which trams once passed.

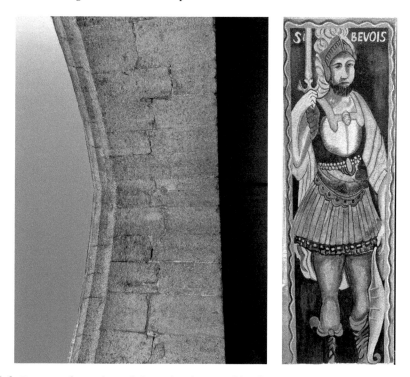

Above left: Green marks on the arch from the electric cables that once powered the tram system.

Above right: Sir Bevois, legendary founder of Southampton.

Old Town Tales

What is today called the Old Town was the main centre of life in medieval times. The town only started to significantly expand with the opening of the docks and the coming of the railways from around 1840.

The defensive Old Town walls were about 1.25 miles long, including seven gates and twenty-nine towers. There is no local stone so everything had to be brought here by boat. Much was picked up by ships stopping at Bembridge on the Isle of Wight, while some better quality stone came from Caen in France.

The thirteenth-century Arundel Tower on the north-west corner was nicknamed Windwhistle Tower. It was about 60 feet high and named after Sir John Arundel, governor of the castle in the late 1300s.

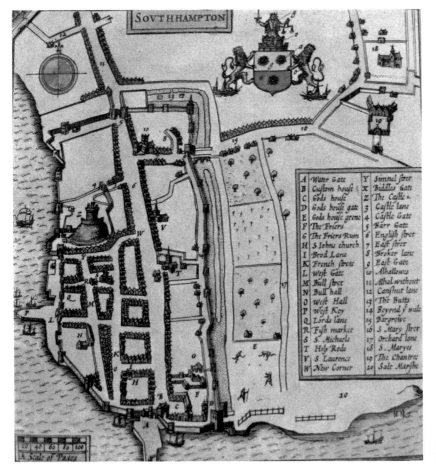

John Speed
map, 1611.

Responsibility for the maintenance and defence of the walls was shared among the various guilds. Around Arundel Tower it was the 'Shoemakers, curriers, sadlers and cobblers'.

The Western Walls would have had the sea lapping up to them. Prince Edward Tower was named after the Black Prince. Also called Catchcold Tower, it has medieval gun ports that are amongst the earliest known examples, dating from the late 1300s.

Throughout the Hundred Years' War, which actually lasted 116 years from 1337 to 1453, there was a constant fear of attack by the French. During this time the walls were reinforced and extended.

The Forty Steps were built in 1851 to provide access to the promenade and foreshore. The Western Esplanade was completed in 1902.

Forest View at the top of the Western Walls dates from around 1820. Today the view of the New Forest is totally obscured.

Above the Undercroft in Bugle Street are two council houses dating from the very early 1900s after slum clearance in the area, possibly the earliest surviving council houses built in England. Like other vaults the Undercroft was used as a wartime air-raid shelter.

Tudor House was once several houses from the early 1400s. Adapted over time, the current frontage, although Tudor in appearance, is a restoration carried out before 1912 when it became Southampton's first museum.

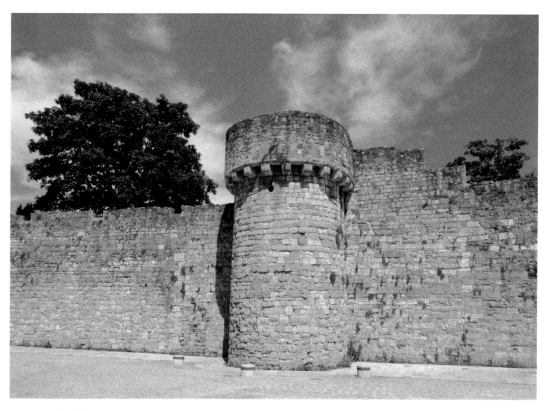

Catchcold Tower.

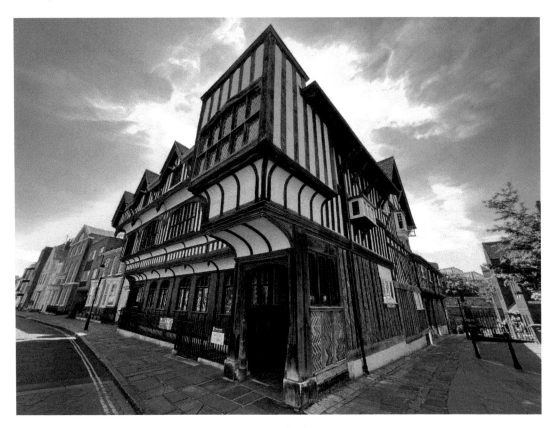

Tudor House with Blue Anchor Lane to the right side of it.

Blue Anchor Lane leads down to one of the original seven town gates. It had many timber-framed houses from which chamber pots were emptied onto unsuspecting people below. At the bottom is possibly the oldest surviving drain cover in Southampton, dating from 1888.

The machicolated Arcades are the only example in England of this style. They are similar to those at the Pope's Palace in Avignon, France.

The West Gate was second only in importance to the Bargate and led to the West Quay where merchant ships arrived. This ordinary looking gate is associated with some key events in history. Edward III and his bowmen used it to embark for France and the Battle of Crecy in 1346. Henry V's fleet mainly left from nearby Portchester, but the king was in Southampton prior to departure. His fleet was only surpassed in size by the one that left for the Normandy beaches in June 1944.

In 1620 the 'Pilgrim Fathers' of sixty-six men, twenty-six women and ten children passed through the West Gate. They took sixty-six days to reach America on the *Mayflower*.

Worshippers at St Michael's Church had to put up with the stench of the fish market right outside the church door. It was moved in 1634 next to the West Gate, where it remains, today called Westgate Hall. The West Gate was complete with 'murder holes' from which punishment was inflicted on those trapped beneath them.

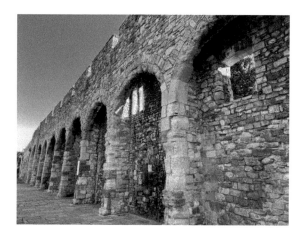

Right: The Arcades date from the late 1300s.

Below: The West Gate.

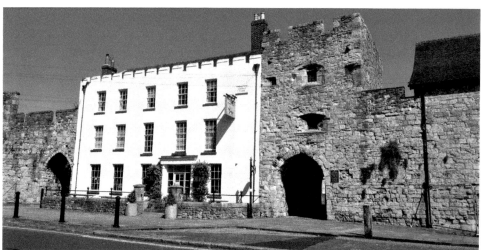

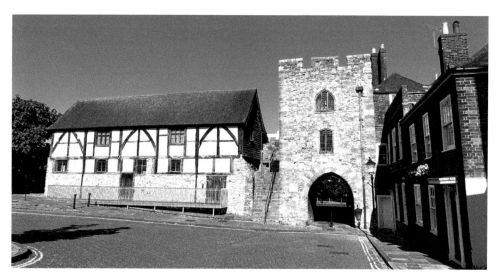

The other side of the West Gate with Westgate Hall to the left.

Opposite Mayflower Park, the Stella Memorial remembers selfless stewardess Mary Anne Rogers of the SS *Stella*. She gave her life jacket to a passenger when the ferry ship was wrecked off the Channel Islands at Easter 1899.

Near the Mayflower Memorial is a sloping wall. In it mysterious large stones, up to 22 inches in diameter, can be seen. No one knows their origin but there are theories. Some say they are cannon balls dredged up from Southampton Water or they are stones intended to be launched by trebuchets when Henry V attacked Harfleur in 1415. Others say they are natural geological formations known as concretions or put there to mark the site of the 1338 French invasion.

The Wool House was built around 1320 as a wool store by the Cistercian monks at Beaulieu Abbey. Wool exports continued until the reign of Henry VIII when it stored alum and spices. Later it acted as a prison for the French and Spanish. Some practised scrimshaw and made model galleons from the bones in their food. Several prisoner names are carved into what is thought to be the longest single span chestnut beam in the country.

Porters Lane was home to ship porters. The large Grade II listed Geddes warehouse dates from 1866. Large goods for ships such as the *Titanic* were stored there, including a Renault car.

At the junction of the High Street and Porters Lane are the remains of the South or Water Gate. Built in 1377, it was mostly demolished in 1804.

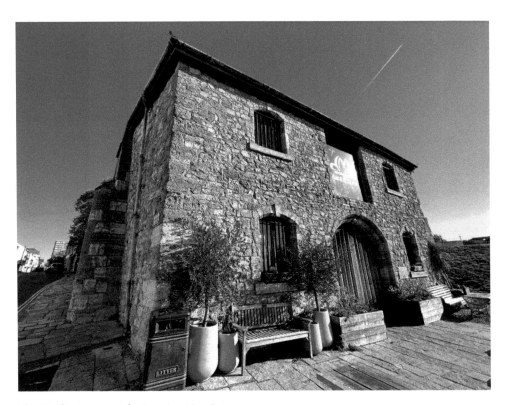

The Wool House, now the Dancing Man Brewery.

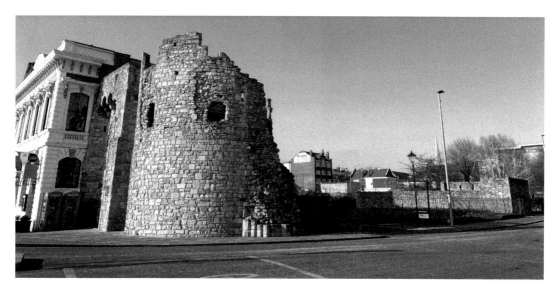

Above: Remains of the Watergate opposite Town Quay.

Right: Tower on the Watergate.

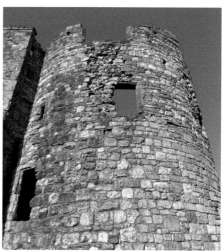

In 1415 it was owned by the Collector of the King's Duties and twice Southampton mayor, William Soper. His will stipulated that the tower house at the gate was leased to a friend from the wealthy Chamberlayne family for an annual rent of one red rose, payable on 24 June, St John the Baptist day. The one condition was that ownership revert to Soper's widow when his friend died.

William was also Keeper of the King's Ships. He built the largest warship of its time, the 1,500-ton *Grace Dieu*, here and it was towed to the Hamble River for fitting out. It was never used, hit by lightning and sank. Some remains can be seen at Bursledon.

INTERESTING EXTRA
The Hamble area was the location for the 1980's TV series *Howards' Way*.

In 1343 much of the south-east part of the Old Town came under royal control. Edward III gave land to his wife Queen Philippa, who endowed it to the newly founded Queen's College, Oxford. It still administers the area today.

In the High Street, the Dolphin Hotel dates back to 1432 and was rebuilt in 1775. The nearby Star Hotel once had a dozen coaches a day leave for London. A young Princess Victoria stayed here when the original Royal Pier was opened.

The failed Southampton Plot to depose Henry V in 1415 led to the trials of the conspirators and their execution at the Bargate. The trial, according to Act II of Shakespeare's Henry V play, took place in the Red Lion pub in the High Street. Its upper level is still called The Courtroom. However, this is very unlikely and it probably took place in Southampton Castle. The beheaded body of the Earl of Cambridge, Henry V's cousin, is said to be buried beneath the altar of St Julien's chapel.

INTERESTING EXTRA
The judge at the trial of Guy Fawkes, the leader of the Gunpowder Plot, was a local man. A descendant of the Fleming family, his verdict led to the execution of Guy Fawkes and his fellow conspirators.

The Eastgate led directly to St Mary's Church, half a mile away, but was demolished in 1775. Polymond Tower on the north-east corner was originally St Denys' Tower, as they were responsible for its maintenance, but it was renamed after a late fourteenth-century mayor.

The north walls are up to 6 feet thick and 20 feet high. In 1769 a gate was made in them called York Gate but due to a low arch it was demolished in 1961.

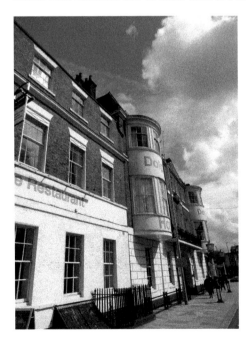

The Dolphin Hotel showing the bay windows. Jane Austen attended balls here.

Sunday, Bloody Sunday

On Sunday 4 October 1338 many townsfolk would have gone to morning mass as usual unaware that fifty galleys from Picardy and Normandy, Spain and Genoa, encouraged by the King of France, were sailing towards the town. The invading fleet had landed near Southampton's West Quay on the Western Esplanade. One of the prime trading ports of King Edward III's England, it was noted for 'wool out and wine in'.

In a day of death and destruction, buildings were set alight, shops and homes looted and the king's own stocks of wine were plundered.

Evidence of a group of skeletons was discovered some years ago in a medieval limekiln in Maddison Street. Some suggest it could be the remains of French raiders from Southampton's fight back.

Their leader Joseph Grimaldi returned to found Monaco. Today, ships marked Grimaldi Lines, owned by the family, are frequent visitors to the nearby container terminal.

King Edward III ordered the Earl of Arundel to discover 'through whose default' Southampton was raided. It was made a garrison town and by February 1339, 100 archers and fifty men-at-arms were posted there. In March 1339, King Edward III himself arrived to inspect the defences. Obviously not satisfied, he ordered the 'enclosing of the town and neighbouring parts with a wall of stone and lime'.

There were walls already and there had been a castle since early Norman times but the West Quay remained open for trade. The Arcades, one of the most striking features of Southampton's old town walls, allowed the merchants to still trade.

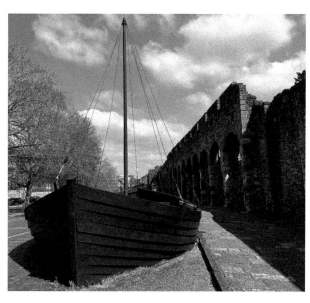

Replica fourteenth-century trading ship on the Western Esplanade.

More medieval vaults remain in Southampton than anywhere else in England. Some estimates say there may have been at least forty-eight. All of the vaults are Scheduled Monuments and protected by Historic England.

The vaults were built primarily for the storage of French red wine sold in casks to the butlers of the aristocracy. They also acted as showrooms to display other imported goods. These are some good remaining examples. No. 94 High Street is one of the largest at 18.1 metres long, 6 metres wide and 2.3 metres high, and was probably built between 1350 and 1400.

Lankester's is on the corner of High Street and West Street. It takes its name from the family who ran the ironworks across the road behind Holy Rood Church. The Undercroft has carvings of heads, possibly of Edward III and his family.

All were later used as air-raid shelters.

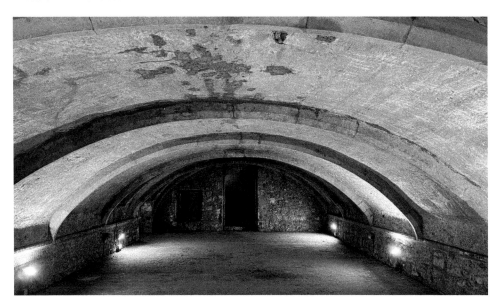

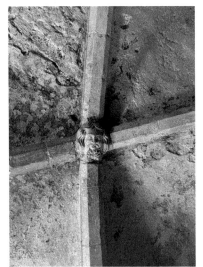

Above: The vault at No. 94 High Street.

Left: Possibly Edward III (1312–77) on the roof of the Undercroft.

Tudor Times

The Tudor House and Garden that is seen today traces its roots back to around 1495, when Sir John Dawtry, an important local official, improved the house with a banqueting hall. The house is central to the history of Southampton and is made up of several houses. Behind Tudor House is the 800-year-old King John's Palace, which is accessible from Tudor House Garden. The name is probably connected to a local merchant and mayor John Wytegod, who had stores there at the time of the 1338 French raid.

During restoration in 2007, conservators discovered that several walls were covered with graffiti dated between 1570 and 1620. Images include ships, caricatures of people and exotic animals. During that period Tudor House was owned by ship owners, so it is likely that the house was used as lodging for sailors and privateers.

After coming close to being demolished in 1886, local philanthropist William Spranger bought the house and led a conservation campaign. It opened as Southampton's first museum on 29 July 1912.

Henry VIII spent time in Southampton, possibly to spend time with Anne Boleyn. The original guidebook names it as King Henry VIII's Palace. In the garden of Tudor House is a large demi culverin cannon originally presented to the king by an Italian merchant in 1542.

The Catholic Philip of Spain arrived in Southampton in 1554 on his way to Winchester to wed Mary Tudor. The half-sister of Elizabeth I, Mary I (1516–58) was also known as 'Bloody Mary' by her Protestant opponents.

'Good Queen Bess' visited Southampton in August 1560 for several days. Elizabeth I visited again in 1569, having ridden from Titchfield where she was entertained by the Earl of Southampton. Elizabeth came for the last time on 4 September 1591 with all her court. The mayor presented her with a gift of £40 from the town. On 7 September, as her entourage was about to leave via the Bargate, members of the 'French Church' met the Queen to express their gratitude. In 1567 Elizabeth had given the Huguenots use of St Julien's Chapel in Winkle Street.

Witchcraft was an issue around this time and Tudor House has markings meant to ward off evil spirits. There was a ducking stool to which women were fastened just east of the Bargate.

In 1579 Widow Walker was accused and searched for markings. In 1594 Widow Wells begged William Hopgood for bread over several days. He reported that some of his pigs behaved strangely then died. She was accused of witchcraft but there are not any records in Southampton of witches being put to death.

The John Speed map of 1611 (shown on page 22), complete with scale and key, gives a good idea of what life was like. His maps were used in the first atlas of Britain. In the upper right-hand corner are the town's coat of arms, given by Elizabeth I in 1575. West Quay and Town Quay are shown, the latter with a crane for loading cargo. At the bottom right are the Admiralty Gallows. John Speed lived in London but his son and his descendants settled in Southampton.

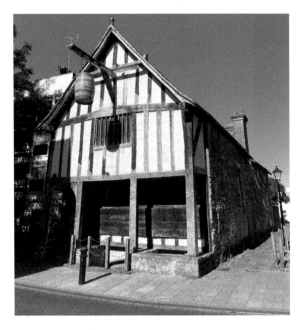

Medieval Merchant's House.

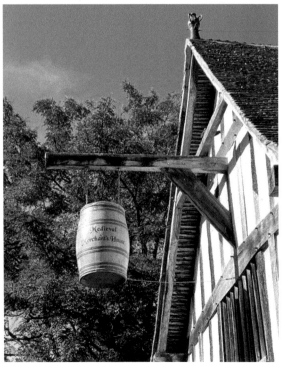

A tun held 1,000 litres of wine.

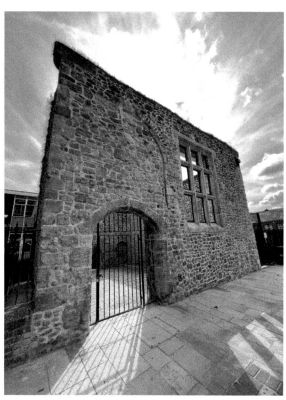

Right: The Weigh House that was
plundered in the 1338 raid.

Below: Weigh House interior.

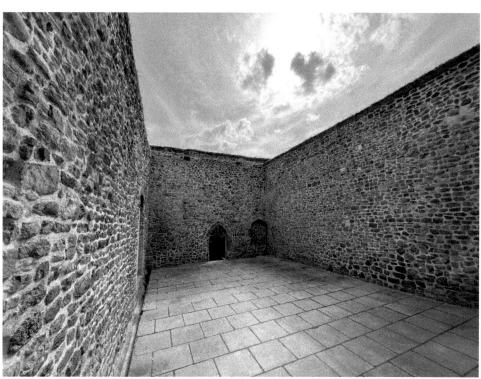

The *Mayflower* Sailed from Southampton

Many will associate the *Mayflower*'s departure with Plymouth. However, Southampton was the intended final departure port for the Settlers and Separatists. The *Mayflower* and the *Speedwell* met in Southampton to load supplies and sail across the Atlantic together.

The two groups of Settlers and Separatists met for the first time in Southampton. The Separatists were Puritans who believed that God could be worshipped wherever a few are gathered in his name. They didn't believe that priests and churches had the monopoly on access to the Almighty. This challenge to the power of the Anglican Church led to their persecution. They had spent some years in the Netherlands but didn't want to put down roots there. A move to the New World across the Atlantic was agreed.

The *Mayflower* arrived from London on 29 July 1620 with Settlers on board. The *Speedwell* arrived a week later with religious Separatists from Leiden in Holland. This was the first time the two groups had met.

For two weeks all necessary provisions were bought in Southampton. Even then, they were still short of ammunition and weapons and had to pay for repairs to the *Speedwell*. They calculated they needed a further £100. Some of the supplies had to be sold to raise money to pay harbour fees and for the *Speedwell*'s repairs.

Thomas Weston arrived with £100 from the Merchant Adventurers to finance the trip. The Separatists were unable to agree to his terms and he returned to London with the money.

Christopher Jones, the master of the *Mayflower*, recruited a young local man, John Alden, to join the crew as a cooper. John looked after the barrels in which food and drink was stored. Alden has a plaque on the Mayflower Memorial.

He married Priscilla Mullins from one of the Pilgrim families and rose to become one of the foremost men of the new colony.

One leading Separatist was William Brewster. Having printed books critical of King James I, his life was in danger and he hid in Southampton, joining the *Speedwell* at the last minute.

INTERESTING EXTRA
Singer Bing Crosby was Brewster's direct descendant.

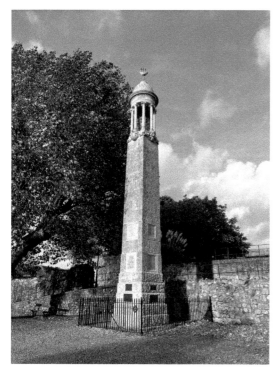
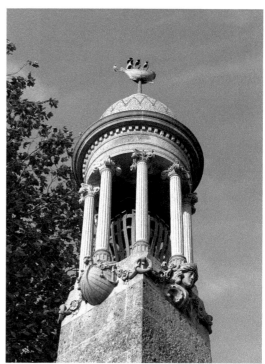

Above left: Mayflower monument.

Above right: The *Mayflower* ship on top of the monument.

Both ships left the Westgate, Southampton, on 16 August 1620. Leaks on the *Speedwell* meant stops at Dartmouth and Plymouth for repairs where it was abandoned. Eighteen people stayed in Plymouth and 102 continued on the *Mayflower*.

Stephen Hopkins came from near Andover, Hampshire. His wife gave birth during the sea journey sometime between leaving Plymouth on 16 September and 19 November 1620 when they arrived at Cape Cod. The boy was named Oceanus.

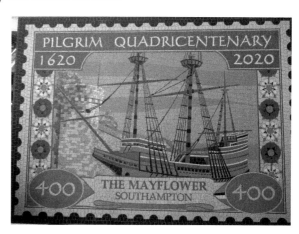

Mayflower mosaic for the 400th anniversary in 2020.

Separatist John Carver had been sent from Leiden to Southampton to organise the buying of supplies. Carver became their first governor in America. His wife brought a letter from John Robinson, their pastor in Holland. It was read to everyone before departure outlining how they needed to all work together. The letter influenced the writing of the Mayflower Compact. This in turn was used as a basis for the American Constitution.

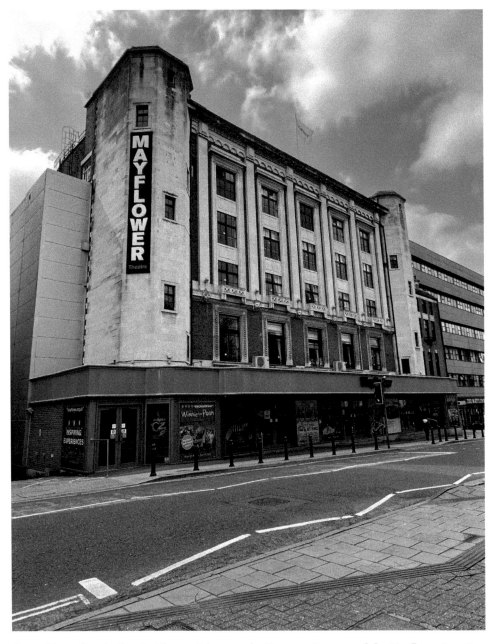

Opened in 1928 as the Empire Theatre, it became the Gaumont in 1950 and the Mayflower in 1987.

The Port of Southampton

Southampton has a unique double tide with up to seventeen hours a day of high water.

The Eastern Docks are now mainly redeveloped as Ocean Village. The foundation stone was laid by Admiral of the Fleet Sir Lucius Curtis on 12 October 1838 on 216 acres of reclaimed mudland. The outer dock opened in 1842 with an inner dock in 1851. In 1890 Queen Victoria opened the Empress Dock.

P&O was the first deep sea line to use the port. The Union Line began a service to South Africa in 1842. The American Line was first to sail transatlantic from 1893, followed by White Star in 1907 and Cunard in 1919.

The White Star Dock was opened in 1911. It changed name to Ocean Dock in 1922 and was used by Cunard. Many older Sotonians fondly recall the impressive art deco Ocean Terminal, which was demolished in 1983.

Flying boats operated passenger and mail services near the Ocean Terminal from 1919 to 1958. A short Sandringham flying boat is in the Solent Sky museum in Albert Road South.

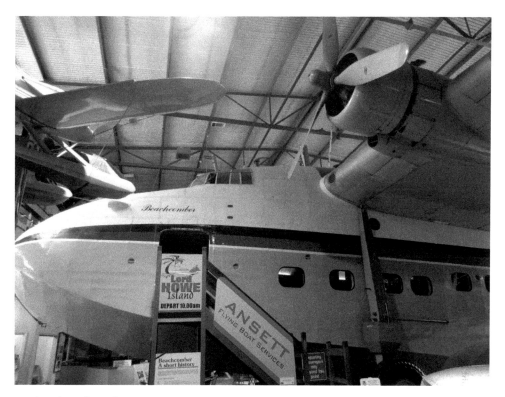

Sandringham flying boat.

The Western Docks, with its 1.5 miles of straight line quay, were started in 1927. It meant reclaiming over 400 acres of land from the sea in the former Western Bay and took until 1934. It could handle the largest ships of its time such as RMS *Queen Elizabeth*. In 1936 the docks handled 46 per cent of the UK's ocean-going passenger traffic.

A temporary floating dry dock, near Town Quay, was in use from 1924. It measured 293 by 41 metres. The King George V Graving Dock replaced it in 1933. It was 365 metres long, 41 metres feet wide and held 58 million gallons of water that could be pumped out in four hours.

The Container Port was opened by Prince Charles in 1968. Today, the five berths are run by DP World and it is the UK's second largest container terminal.

Mayflower Park, between the docks and the former Royal Pier, is one of the few public places to view our busy port. The original wooden pier from 1833 was replaced with an iron one in 1895.

The port supports many jobs and contributes £2.5 billion to the nation's economy every year. It is the UK's number one export port handling goods worth £40 billion annually. It is the UK's number one vehicle handling port, processing 900,000 vehicles annually.

As Europe's leading turnaround cruise port, Southampton welcomes around 2 million passengers annually to its five cruise terminals. The new Horizon Cruise Terminal has the UK's first ship to shore power facility for cruise ships.

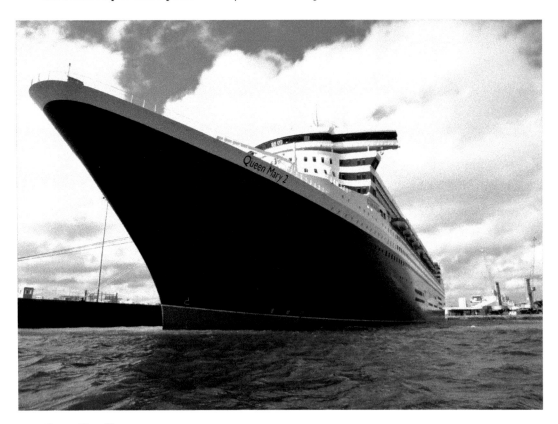

Queen Mary II.

A Coat of Many Colours

As a port, Southampton has a long history of immigration from other parts of the world. It recorded the third-highest number of 'aliens', as they were called, as a percentage of the local population in England in 1377.

An African carpenter known as Black John settled in the town in 1492. Jacques Francis, an African salvage diver, led a team tasked with salvaging valuables from two merchant ships that sank near Southampton and a 1546 attempt to salvage the *Mary Rose*.

Huguenots refugees settled here in the sixteenth century. St Julien's, the 'French church', in Winkle Street still only has one annual service in English every July.

Although Southampton was not a hub for the transatlantic slave trade in the same way that Bristol or Liverpool were, many of its residents prospered from the exploitation of enslaved people, particularly in the Caribbean. There is no evidence of actual slaves passing through the port but ships and sailors based here went on to transport slaves from Africa to the sugar plantations in the Caribbean or the cotton fields in the USA. Some slave owners such as Thomas Combes and John Morant, lived locally, owning plantations from Sumatra in Indonesia to the West Indies.

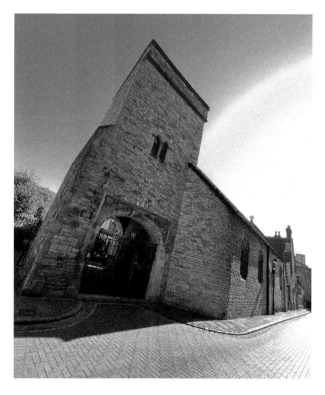

St Julien's or the French Church in Winkle Street.

There is a painting by Maria Spilsbury from around 1800 which shows Anthony de Source and his son working as black servants at a New Year's Day feast given by engineer Walter Taylor for his 100 employees.

A map exists of a sugar plantation in Nevis, owned by a Southampton resident. There was the Sugar House in Gloucester Square, where Caribbean sugar cane was processed for use locally.

Of mixed-race descent, Ann Middleton was born in Jamaica. She married Nathaniel Middlelton, a rich East India Company merchant. He created Townhill Park Estate *c.*1787, which she inherited on his death. Today the Gregg Independent School is on the site.

Southampton did have extensive trading links with the West Indies. Some former West Indian planters and merchants had retired to the town and surrounding areas. At the Audit House in January 1824, a petition in support of the government's proposals to improve the conditions of slaves in the West Indies was defeated. The *Southampton Herald* reported that all the nobility and gentry of the town had attended the meeting and voted against.

In March 1825 a Southampton branch of the Anti-Slavery Society was set up and in 1828 around 1,400 locals signed a petition to end slavery. In 1834, Parliament abolished slavery in the British West Indies. In 1839 the British and Foreign Anti-Slavery Society (BFASS) was established in London with the aim of abolishing slavery worldwide, particularly in the United States. In 1840 the Southampton Anti-Slavery Society became a branch of the BFASS. Prominent in the local branch were Thomas Adkins, Minister of the Above Bar Congregational Church, Edward Palk, a High Street chemist, and George Laishley, a Methodist and a draper.

Southampton sent five delegates to the World Anti-Slavery Convention in 1843. The anti-slavery movement in the town declined after the abolition of slavery in the United States in 1862.

The Reverend Thomas A Pinckney (1809–1887) was born in South Carolina, a southern slave state and ordained in 1852. By 1858 he was in London at the Colonial Church and School Society. He was sent to Quebec province where many were fugitive slaves and established a school. On 29 February 1860 he married Elizabeth King, a white English missionary. Some handbills described this interracial marriage as 'this violation of the

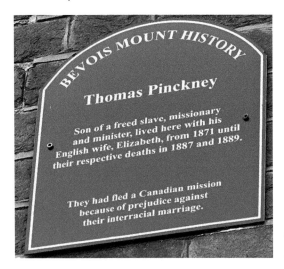

Thomas Pinckney plaque in Avenue Road.

law of God, and our common nature'. The couple resigned their missionary posts. Moving to Southampton, in the 1871 census they were at Brent Cottage, Avenue Road, where they lived quietly until their respective deaths.

The most common reason for immigration was trade. Merchants from the Low Countries often brought materials crucial to the textile industry, including alum and woad both used in cloth-making.

Merchants from Italy, who comprised the largest group among Southampton's immigrant population, regularly brought spices including pepper, ginger and saffron.

Export of English wool accounted for 90 per cent of English trade during the reign of Henry VII (1485–1509). It was exported through Southampton more often than any other port.

The impact that immigrant merchants had on Southampton is shown by the response to the Hosting Act of 1439, introduced to curtail the activities of foreign merchants. They now had to declare themselves to local authorities upon arrival, in order to be assigned an English 'host' who would supervise their business transactions. To persuade English merchants to volunteer as hosts, the Act stipulated that an English merchant could take two pence in every pound's worth of merchandise sold by the foreign merchant.

However, Southampton's civic officials treated the Hosting Act as nothing more than a formality as the city's economic prosperity depended on foreign merchants being able to trade freely. Alien merchants remained able to rent their own houses, whereas the Hosting Act required that they lived in the same property as their designated host.

Southampton's immigrant population was often wealthy. Merchant John Le Fleming became mayor and MP and his statue is on the north wall in Bargate Street.

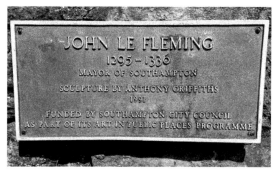

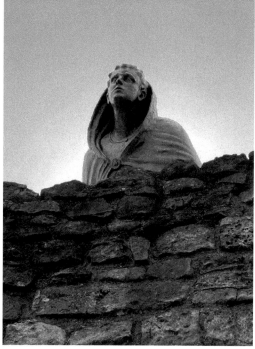

Above: The Fleming statue and plaque is between the Bargate and Arundel Tower.

Right: John Le Fleming was a wealthy Flemish merchant.

In the 1370s, immigrants could apply for 'letters of denization' which granted them a form of citizenship that gave the right to own property.

William Overeye, an Irish immigrant, was twice mayor of Southampton before becoming the Member of Parliament in 1426. A Venetian, Damiano de Pezaro, stated in 1438 that after fifteen years as a resident he had been honoured with appointment as a 'freeman of the city'. Another Venetian, Gabriel Corbizzi, served as a steward of the city in the 1440s.

Christopher Ambrose came from Florence and was mayor in 1486 and 1497. Hostility to Italians in London drove many to relocate to Southampton in the mid-1400s. Merchants from Genoa provided two-thirds of the city's petty customs revenue in 1451.

In 1868, an Australian touring cricket team, composed entirely of indigenous players, played Hampshire at Hoglands Park. After the drawn game they put on a display of boomerang throwing. The West Indian cricket team toured England in 1900, arriving in Southampton with two black professional players, Float Woods and Tommie Burton. They won against Hampshire at the County Ground in Northlands Road.

Ships to call at Southampton carrying West Indian migrants in the 1940s include the *Almanzora*, in December 1947.

Black History Month has been held since 2005 in Southampton. Plaques remember events such as when Bob Marley played at the Coach House Inn at the rear of the Fleming Arms on 29 May 1973.

Mae Street Kidd was the Red Cross Director of Services for black American soldiers in Southampton during the Second World War. Her plaque is at the Royal South Hants Hospital. Craig David has a plaque above The Painted Wagon venue. The Ebony Rockers mural in Above Bar Street includes his father, George David.

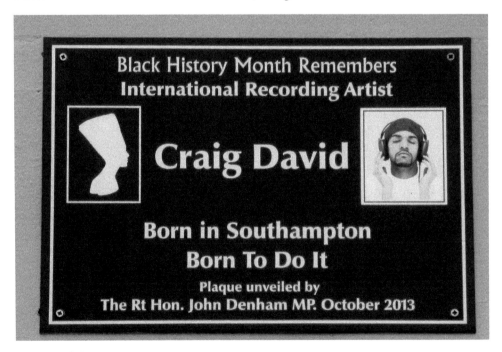

Craig David plaque.

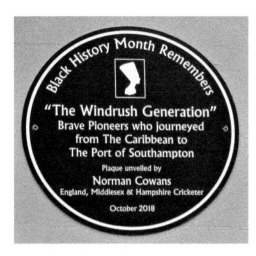

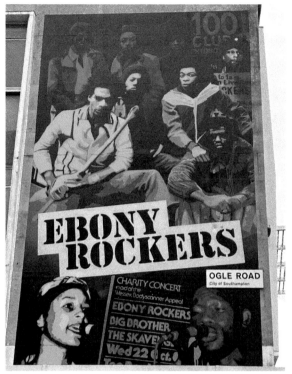

Above: The Windrush Generation.

Right: Ebony Rockers mural near The Marlands Shopping Centre. Craig David's father was a member of this reggae band.

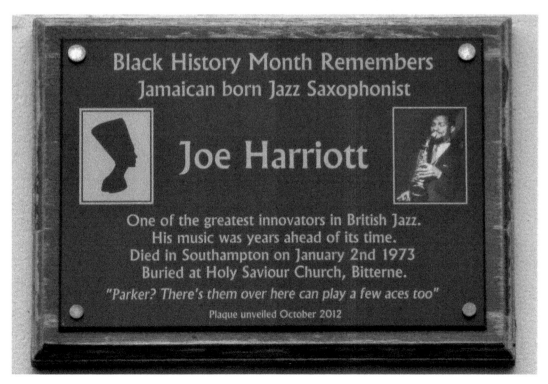

Jazz saxophonist Joe Harriott.

Southampton's Jewel in the Crown

The City Council lists fifty-six parks and open spaces, eight greenways and twenty-three allotment sites. Southampton has an estimated 267,000 trees, one per resident. The 52 acres of the central parks and the 365-acre Common are Southampton's 'Jewel in the Crown', the lungs of our city.

The five parks are called West or Watts, East or Andrews, Palmerston, Houndwell and Hoglands. The parks were created from the Lammas Lands. 'Lammas' derives from 'loaf mass', a mid-August ceremony that celebrated the bringing in of corn.

When the marshland from God's House Tower to the shore of the River Itchen was sold for the eastern docks, these Lammas Lands were purchased with the proceeds. The parks were laid out from 1854 to 1866. The Victorians believed fresh air and open spaces were good for the mind, body and soul.

Southampton-born hymn writer Isaac Watts (1678–1748) has a statue in Watts Park. He was educated at King Edward VI Grammar School. His 'O God our Help In Ages Past' based on Psalm 19 is the school hymn to this day. The tune is chimed on the Civic Centre clock tower at 8 a.m., noon and 4 p.m. daily.

He penned many popular hymns such as 'There is a Land of Pure Delight'. His inspiration was the view from the Town Walls across the River Test to the New Forest,

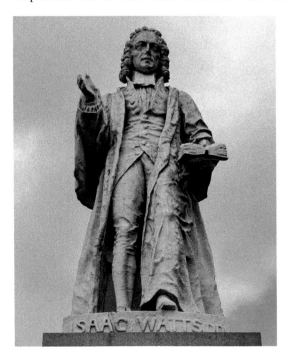

Isaac Watts statue in Watts Park.

which reminded him of the River Jordan with Canaan on the opposite bank. The Cenotaph was designed by Sir Edwin Luytens, who also designed the national one in Whitehall. It has an empty tomb atop. The parks have plants from all over the world – even a black stemmed bamboo in East Park.

The Alpine Rock garden, built in the 1930s, may contain remnants of the Stag Gates on the Avenue that were removed in 1919.

The Richard Andrews statue remembers a five-time mayor. Known as Southampton's Dick Whittington, he arrived impoverished but went on to run a successful carriage-making business. One was used by Queen Victoria at Osborne House on the Isle of Wight. He never forgot his humble origins and was a benevolent employer.

In 1862 Frederick Perkins presented the impressive lime tree avenue that runs through East, Palmerston and Houndwell parks. The trees are planted old by new so that as one dies a new one is planted and the line remains constant. In February 2023, Princess Anne planted a tree in East Park.

Palmerston Park is noted for its rhododendrons, azaleas and magnolias. It has a statue of former PM the 3rd Viscount Palmerston, who was a burgess of the town. He lived on the Broadlands estate at nearby Romsey.

Houndwell has the Charles Melly drinking fountain dated 1859. Melly, a rich Liverpuddlian merchant and philanthropist, worked with local Unitarian minister Edmund Kell to provide free clean water to stop the poor from drinking excess alcohol. The 50-feet-high Chamberlayne Gas Column recalls William Chamberlyne MP who provided gas lighting to the town in 1820. He also owned the company that supplied the gas.

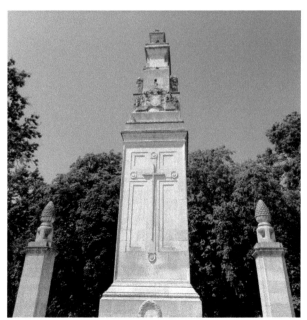
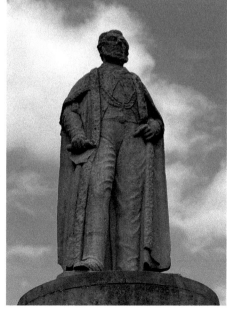

Above left: The Cenotaph.

Above right: Richard Andrews statue in East Park.

46

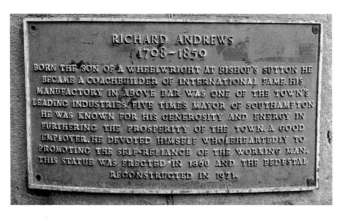

RICHARD ANDREWS
1798~1859

BORN THE SON OF A WHEELWRIGHT AT BISHOP'S SUTTON HE
BECAME A COACHBUILDER OF INTERNATIONAL FAME. HIS
MANUFACTORY IN ABOVE BAR WAS ONE OF THE TOWN'S
LEADING INDUSTRIES. FIVE TIMES MAYOR OF SOUTHAMPTON
HE WAS KNOWN FOR HIS GENEROSITY AND ENERGY IN
FURTHERING THE PROSPERITY OF THE TOWN. A GOOD
EMPLOYER. HE DEVOTED HIMSELF WHOLEHEARTEDLY TO
PROMOTING THE SELF-RELIANCE OF THE WORKING MAN.
THIS STATUE WAS ERECTED IN 1860 AND THE PEDESTAL
RECONSTRUCTED IN 1971.

Southampton's 'Dick Whittington'.

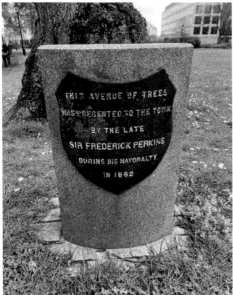

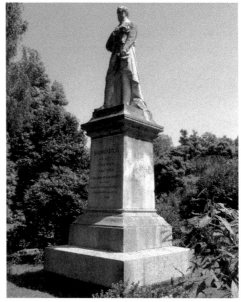

Above left: Mayor Perkins presented the Lime Tree Avenue in 1862.

Above right: Lord Palmerston was a burgess of Southampton.

Left: Chamberlayne column in Houndwell Park. He donated gas lamps to the town in 1820.

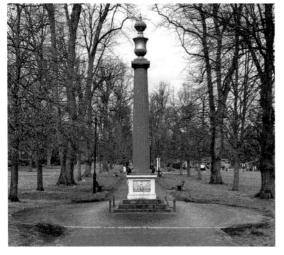

Hoglands Park has a plaque to people who died when a bomb directly landed on an air-raid shelter there in 1940. Speakers Corner was created on the edge of Hoglands Park following the initial pedestrianisation of Above Bar Street in August 1971. Rarely used, it is redundant since the advent of social media.

The Common, a Site of Special Scientific Interest, was designated as common land in 1228. This allowed all householders within the borough to use the land for grazing, fuel, clay, and taking berries and other wild, natural food.

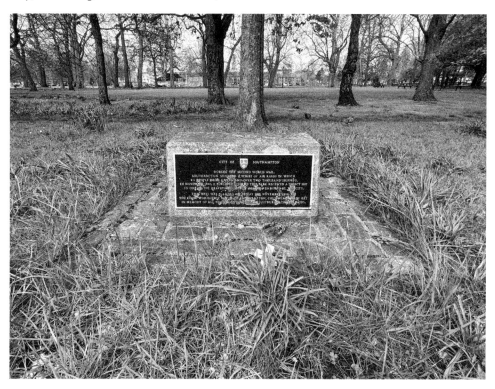

Above: In Hoglands Park.

Right: In East Park, remembering locals who died in the Clapham Rail Disaster 1988.

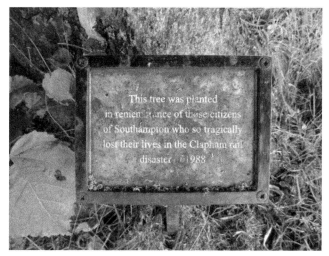

The site of an eighteenth-century brickworks, Hawthorn Cottage was purchased by the council in 1945 and demolished. Miss Newman lived there, the 'Lady on the Bike' who distributed the Titanic Relief Fund by cycle until her death in 1940. It then became Southampton Zoo in 1961 run by the Chipperfield family. Today it is hard to imagine that James the Smoking Chimp was once a popular attraction. Poor conditions at the zoo led to protests in the early 1980s, some led by Joanna Lumley, and the zoo closed in 1985. In 1999 Mary Chipperfield was found guilty on twelve counts of animal cruelty and fined £85,000. The council used the site to make the Hawthorns Urban Wildlife Centre.

The Avenue, a straight road from Southampton towards Winchester, runs through the Common and is based on an old Roman route. Trees were planted on either side to commemorate the English victory at the 1745 Battle of Culloden against the Scots.

So why is the well-known Cowherds pub so-called? As well as looking after the cattle, it was the cowherd's job to perform maintenance on the gates, fences and banks on the Common. In the 1600s the cowherd was paid two pennies per cow but was required to pay rent for a house. The job of cowherd was kept in the same family from generation to generation. In 1762 the cowherd's house was rebuilt at the expense of Alderman William Knight, who agreed to pay for the building on the condition that the rent (which was then raised to £6 a year) was distributed among the poor of Southampton's parishes. In order to meet this higher rent the cowherd began to sell alcoholic drinks. In 1789 the cowherd's house was leased by the town council to a firm of brewers as an inn.

The town gallows were once located on the north of Southampton Common, near Bassett crossroads, with the last public execution taking place there in July 1785.

A racecourse was built on the Common in 1822 and races continued to be held until 1881. In 1874 the council gave permission for a golf course to be constructed.

In 1843 10 acres were split off by Southampton Corporation to be used as a cemetery, opened in 1846. The Old Cemetery still has some burials but only if you have an existing family plot. It contains over sixty graves of local people connected to the *Titanic* but none of those who perished in the actual sinking.

In 1835 the Southampton Waterworks commissioners decided to build an artesian well on the Common. By 1883 it reached a depth of 1,317 feet (401 metres) but it never really worked. Our water then came from the Waterworks at Twyford and still does.

In 1892 a small hospital was built for cholera and smallpox cases. It was, however, unsuitable so the council purchased the City of Adelaide ship to use as an Isolation Hospital, anchored off Millbrook Point. The Adelaide Medical Centre in Millbrook is named after the ship.

During the First World War much of the Common was taken over by the military for a rest camp. During the Second World War the Common was again used by the military as a prisoner of war camp was also set up.

The Southampton Show started in 1952. In 1988 the show transitioned into the Balloon & Flower Festival and ceased after 2005.

In 1968 the council proposed to construct two car parks on the Common. This proposal was successfully challenged in the High Court by Edward Chalk of the Southampton Commons and Parks Protection Society. There is a plaque to him in Palmerston Park.

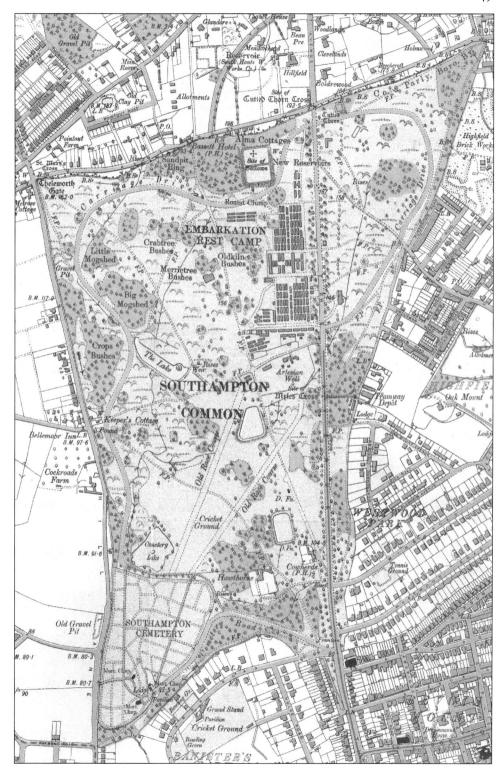

The First World War map of the Common.

15

How a Father and Son Helped Defeat Napoleon

In October 1805 during the Napoleonic Wars Admiral Nelson engaged thirty-eight Spanish and French ships off the coast of Spain near Cape Trafalgar. Nelson had a plan which involved splitting the enemy line into three and engaging the middle third, which included their flag ship, in close combat. This was a break with traditional naval tactics at the time and Nelson needed to be confident about the manoeuvrability of his ships and their firepower. Nelson's plan succeeded and ended Napoleon's plans to invade Britain. The British had destroyed nineteen enemy ships and killed or wounded 6,000 French and Spanish men.

Nelson's success at Trafalgar was in part due to the skill and expertise of a Southampton father and son both called Walter Taylor. In 1734 Walter Taylor, a skilled ship's carpenter, and his wife Elizabeth had a son they named Walter. Young Walter was indentured as an apprentice to a ship's pulley block maker, in Westgate Street, when he was fourteen years old.

His father spent time researching the manufacturer of ships' pulley blocks. They were not very reliable as they were individually handmade, prone to snagging and jamming. Ships relied on the pulley blocks to control the sails and to position cannons for firing from the gun ports. In 1754, the Taylors bought a block making business and developed sawing, boring and turning machinery to mass produce them to great accuracy and quality. The Taylor's blocks were successfully tested by the Navy, who then bought all of their output. A seventy-four-gun warship needed 1,400 such blocks.

The father died in 1762 and young Walter continued the business to produce blocks for the Admiralty. The business expanded and later moved to Mayfield Park in Southampton where a stream provided the power for the machinery. Now producing 100,000 blocks a year for the Navy in 1781, the business moved to Woodmill where the river provided more power and was supplemented by steam engines.

Walter lived in Portswood on the site of the current library and was a philanthropic employer setting up a school for his employees' children.

The efficiency and reliability of Walter's blocks together with the skill of the British seamen meant that Nelson's ships had far greater manoeuvrability. Also each British cannon could fire as many as four volleys to the enemy's one at the same time.

Walter died in 1803 and was buried at South Stoneham church.

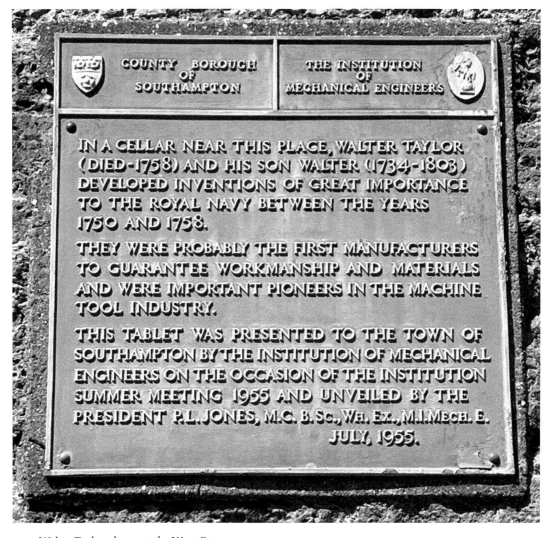

COUNTY BOROUGH OF SOUTHAMPTON

THE INSTITUTION OF MECHANICAL ENGINEERS

IN A CELLAR NEAR THIS PLACE, WALTER TAYLOR (DIED-1758) AND HIS SON WALTER (1734-1803) DEVELOPED INVENTIONS OF GREAT IMPORTANCE TO THE ROYAL NAVY BETWEEN THE YEARS 1750 AND 1758.

THEY WERE PROBABLY THE FIRST MANUFACTURERS TO GUARANTEE WORKMANSHIP AND MATERIALS AND WERE IMPORTANT PIONEERS IN THE MACHINE TOOL INDUSTRY.

THIS TABLET WAS PRESENTED TO THE TOWN OF SOUTHAMPTON BY THE INSTITUTION OF MECHANICAL ENGINEERS ON THE OCCASION OF THE INSTITUTION SUMMER MEETING 1955 AND UNVEILED BY THE PRESIDENT P.L. JONES, M.C. B.Sc., Wh. Ex., M.I.MECH. E.
JULY, 1955.

Walter Taylor plaque at the West Gate.

16

A Licence to Print Money

Our area has fast-flowing chalk streams providing energy and water for papermaking. In 1700 there were 10 paper mills in Hampshire, nine making brown paper and one on the Itchen at South Stoneham near Southampton manufacturing white paper. This is known today as Gater's Mill at Mansbridge just beyond the White Swan pub. It was here that the young Huguenot Henri de Portal learned the skill of white papermaking.

About sixty people, many of French origin, would have been employed at South Stoneham. It was one of several mills in England operated by the Company of White Paper Makers. It formed when fifteen men, nine of whom had French Protestant roots, were granted a patent and then a charter by James II enabling them to make writing and printing paper. Of the nine French Huguenots, five had connections in Southampton where most were burgesses and businessmen rather than skilled papermakers. One, Elias de Grouchy, became a Mayor of Southampton.

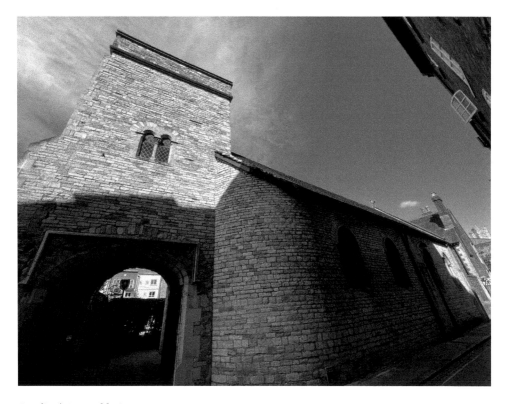

St Julien's in Winkle Street.

During the late seventeenth and early eighteenth centuries French Protestants known as Huguenots were persecuted and many fled to nearby countries. One fifteen-year-old French Huguenot was Henri de Portal. Legend has it he escaped to Southampton hidden inside a wine barrel with his brother. Arriving in Southampton around 1705, he attended the French Church in Winkle Street.

His wealthy family originated from Toulouse and a key papermaker at South Stoneham, Gerard de Vaux, was also from Toulouse. Gerard obtained work for Henri at South Stoneham where he learned the art of papermaking. In 1711 Henri was naturalised at Winchester Quarter Sessions. The certificate described him as 'Henry Portal, of South Stoneham, Gentleman'.

Henri made friends with Sir William Heathcote, who leased him Bere Mill near Whitchurch in 1711. In 1718 Henry leased Laverstoke Mill further up the Test making paper for the Indian rupee. In 1724 Henry was awarded the contract to produce paper for banknotes by Sir Gilbert Heathcote, the Governor of the Bank of England and uncle of Henry's friend Sir William Heathcote. Henry's particular expertise was the production of paper with superb watermarks essential for security with paper money.

17

Southampton's Spa Town Days (1750–1830)

Many are surprised to learn that Southampton was once a popular spa town. Few traces survive, although there is still a Spa Road.

In 1723, the Earl of Peterborough, a supporter of the Protestant royals William and Mary, had built Bevois Mount House on 50 acres just north of Lodge Road. It was believed this was where local legendary hero Sir Bevois of Hamtun was buried. The earl's retirement to Bevois Mount came after his second marriage to the famous opera singer Anastasia Robinson.

A regular guest to Bevois Mount House was the earl's friend the poet Alexander Pope. Pope said of Southampton: 'Its air is salubrious, the scenery in the neighbourhood fine and its society very select'.

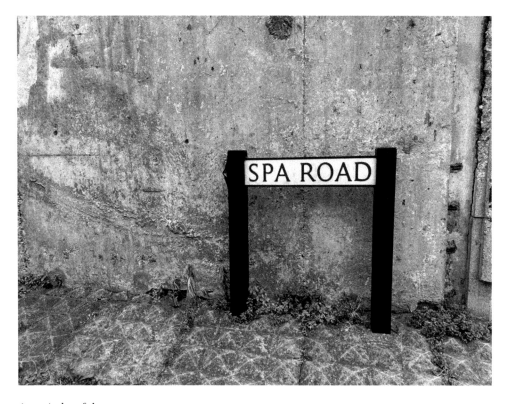

A reminder of the spa town era.

INTERESTING EXTRA
Henry and Sophia Hulton lived at Bevois Mount House from 1808 to 1840. They are ancestors of former Prime Minister David Cameron.

During the eighteenth century, writers were reporting that the Southampton air was ideal for people suffering from respiratory diseases. The air was free of dampness as the gravel on which the town was built drained very quickly. The sea spray-laden air was said to be excellent for healthy teeth as shown by the teeth of the local women who collected shells along the shore.

Many wealthy families purchased large tracts of land in the locality and developed estates with grand houses. William Chamberlayne's home at Weston Grove overlooked Southampton Water.

In 1750 Frederick, Prince of Wales, was in the area and swam in the Test, then quenched his thirst by drinking water from the chalybeate spring. He was so taken by the invigorating effect that his family became regular visitors to the town.

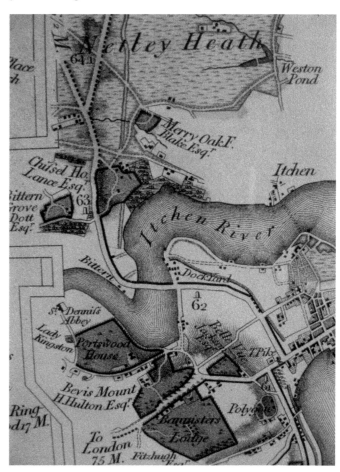

Map showing some of the important houses.

Analysis of Southampton's chalybeate spring water showed it to be more beneficial than that of Tunbridge Wells and the spa town era started. Many benefits were claimed for the water including the treatment of eczema, constipation, leprosy, rheumatism, palsy and rickets.

Royalty including George III, the aristocracy and the wealthy converged on Southampton for the benefits of the sea, the air and the healing waters. Among regular visitors were the Dukes of Gloucester, York and Cumberland. Royal Navy officers lived in the town preferring the social life of Southampton with the opportunities it provided for potential marriage to women from influential families.

To cater for the visitors the New Rooms were built at the end of Bargate Street. A fountain was installed so that the chalybeate spring water could be consumed. In more recent times, a private local hospital and the Close it was in were named the Chalybeate, but is now Spire Southampton Hospital.

The New Rooms were renamed the Archery Rooms when the Royal Southampton Archers were formed in 1789 with the Duke of Gloucester as their patron. They eventually moved to land off The Avenue where the eponymous Archers Lodge and Archers Road were later constructed.

Sea baths were constructed at the end of Simnel Street, near Cross House on the Itchen and on what was then known as The Beach where Union Castle House is today. Special platforms with slatted adjustable bottoms that could be adjusted according to the tide were installed.

When not bathing or drinking the water, visitors could take part in card games, visit the coffee shops in the High Street or visit one of the many bookshops and lending libraries established for their use. One was operated by Thomas Baker in the High Street with nearly 7,000 volumes. Sailing was popular, with regular regattas organised, as was horse racing, which took place at Stoneham and on the Common.

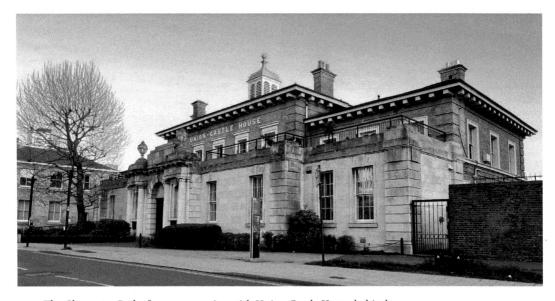

The Gloucester Baths frontage remains with Union Castle House behind.

Thomas Baker printed a map of the area 10 miles round Southampton together with a guidebook so that having hired a horse or a carriage the visitor could explore the area.

Promenading was also popular and the path to Crosshouse, now Canute Road, was landscaped for this purpose. For evening entertainment dances and balls with strict etiquette rules took place at venues such as the Dolphin Hotel.

In 1766 the Theatre Royal playhouse was constructed in French Street, modelled on the theatre in Covent Garden and paid for by subscription. It attracted leading actors such as Charles Kean, David Garrick and Sarah Siddons.

During the spa period two Pavement Commissioners' Acts were passed giving powers to improve the town in terms of lighting, security, building construction and cleanliness. The Commissioners were not popular as they could raise rates to fund their work.

New accommodation was needed to oversee the administration of the expanding town. The medieval Audit House near Holyrood Church was in poor repair. A site in the High Street was purchased on which a new Audit House was constructed from September 1771. It was destroyed by bombing during the Second World War and the administration moved to the newly constructed Civic Centre, completed in 1939.

Many of the hotels in the High Street were redeveloped to cater for the spa visitors and we can still enjoy the Georgian frontage of the Star and the Dolphin Hotels.

Southampton's importance as a spa town began to wane at the beginning of the nineteenth century as Brighton's popularity drew visitors away. Nearby there are many fine houses constructed towards the end of the spa period by Samuel Toomer for the wealthy. Good examples can be seen along Carlton Crescent.

An 1809 statue of King George III, dressed as the Emperor Hadrian in a niche on the south of the Bargate, serves as a permanent reminder that his siblings were regular visitors during Southampton's spa town era.

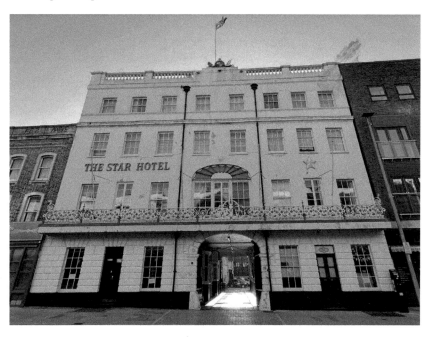

The Star Hotel in the High Street.

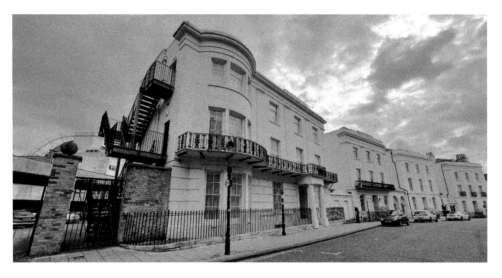

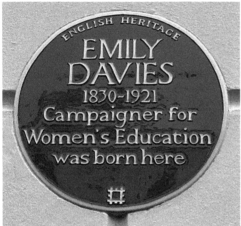

Above: Carlton Crescent.

Left: Emily Davies co-founded Girton College, Cambridge.

General Henry Shrapnel retired to Southampton in 1830, first living at a house in Bugle Street and then at Peartree House where he died in 1842. In 1784, while a lieutenant in the Royal Artillery, he invented a hollow cannon ball filled with shot which burst in mid-air. Adopted by the British Army in 1803, it acquired the inventor's name as the shrapnel shell. Its use was crucial in the Battle of Waterloo and Shrapnel was awarded a lifetime pension in 1815.

In 1600, a group of London merchants had petitioned Queen Elizabeth I for a royal charter to trade with the countries of the eastern hemisphere. And so, the 'Honourable Company of Merchants of London Trading with the East Indies', or East India Company (EIC), was founded. 258 years later, the company would pass control of the Indian subcontinent to the British crown.

Some who had made their fortune as army officers with the EIC were involved with the Polygon scheme of the 1760s. The idea was to build a safe, upmarket area for wealthy people to the north of the Old Town. This ambitious plan was designed to match the refined buildings of other spa or resort towns like Bath and Tunbridge Wells.

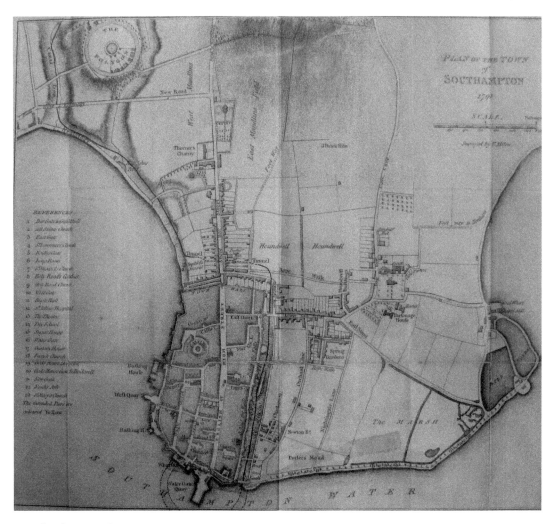

Southampton in 1791.

The idea was conceived by Isaac Mallortie and John Carnac, who commissioned the architect Jacob Leroux to draw up plans. The original plan of *c.* 1768 was for a polygonal ensemble covering about 22 acres and consisting, within an encircling carriage road, of twelve large houses with long gardens, assembly rooms and a hotel. Lack of money caused the scheme to be aborted by 1773. A later Polygon Hotel, incorporating some of the original, was on the site until 1999. In its day it was the premier hotel where visiting celebrities stayed.

18

Jane Austen

(1775–1817)

In 1806 newly married Francis Austen was in the Navy. He suggested that his wife Mary, his mother, sisters Jane and Cassandra and Martha Lloyd should share a house together. Southampton was a good choice because it was near to Portsmouth, where Frank was based.

Author Jane had been to Southampton twice previously. First when she was seven to attend Mrs Cawley's school near the Bargate with sister Cassandra. Southampton as a busy port was often one of the first places that diseases and infections from abroad would first take hold. Sister Cassandra, cousin Jane Cooper and the young Jane became ill with fever. The second time Jane stayed in Southampton was when she was eighteen. She stayed with her cousin Elizabeth Austen, who had married money and moved to the St Mary's Street area. Jane and Cassandra attended a ball at the Dolphin Hotel. The last time Jane lived here was from 1806 to 1809.

A mock-Tudor pub, the Juniper Berry, is on the site of the house today. Jane enjoyed the fact that the house in Castle Square had a garden, something she had not been able to enjoy when living in Bath. Jane mentions getting a laburnum and having gooseberry bushes and raspberries planted.

Jane refers to 'The Beach' in her letters. This was a stretch of land that bordered the Itchen River between the Town Quay and Cross House. A shelter still stands, built to shield passengers waiting to be rowed across by ferrymen from the Itchen Ferry community situated on the Woolston side of the river.

The gateway through God's House Tower would have been the entrance through which Jane and her family accessed The Beach. Netley Abbey was a popular place for the Austens to visit.

Some locals did not make a good impression on Jane. Mrs Lance, who lived at Chessel House, Bitterne, was not approved of. Two of the local roads, Lances Hill and Little Lances Hill, remind us of the Lance family. In 1807 Jane wrote to her sister Cassandra, who was at Godmersham: 'We found only Mrs Lance at home ... She was civil and chatty enough, and offered to introduce us to acquaintances in Southampton, which we gratefully declined. They live in a handsome style and are rich, and she seemed to like to be rich. We gave her to understand we were far from being so; she will soon feel therefore that we are not worth her acquaintance.'

One, maybe slightly salacious story emerges while Jane, Martha and her mother are in Southampton. Jane relates a relationship between Dr Mant, the rector of All Saints

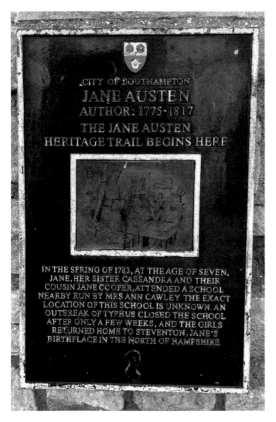 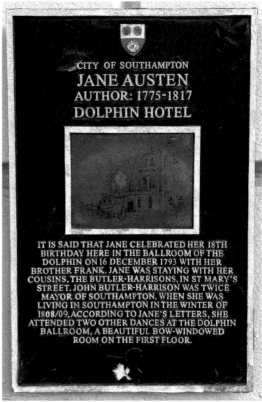

Above left: Start of the Jane Austen Trail, south side of the Bargate.

Above right: Jane had her eighteenth birthday at the Dolphin Hotel.

Church in the High Street, and Martha Lloyd. Dr Mant had been the headmaster of King Edward VI Grammar School. In Jane's day, the grammar school was in French Street, close to Castle Square. Dr Mant had also been a professor of divinity at Oxford, written religious discussion pamphlets and was a charismatic preacher. He had a following of young ladies including Martha.

On Tuesday 17 January 1809 Jane wrote to Cassandra: 'Martha & Dr Mant are as bad as ever; he runs after her in the street to apologise for having spoken to a Gentleman while she was near him the day before. – Poor Mrs Mant can stand it no longer; she is retired to one of her married Daughters.'

The Dolphin Hotel, which still stands today, was the venue for balls in Jane's time. Today the first floor room is named after Jane. After a winter ball Jane wrote to sister Cassandra in December 1808: 'The room was tolerably full & there were perhaps thirty couples of dancers. The melancholy part was to see so many dozen young women standing by without partners & each of them with two ugly naked shoulders!'

Also within easy walking distance of Castle Square was Southampton's main theatre, the Theatre Royal, which Jane attended.

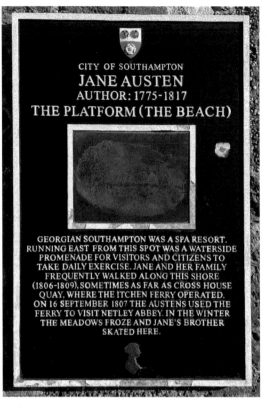

CITY OF SOUTHAMPTON
JANE AUSTEN
AUTHOR: 1775-1817
THE PLATFORM (THE BEACH)

GEORGIAN SOUTHAMPTON WAS A SPA RESORT.
RUNNING EAST FROM THIS SPOT WAS A WATERSIDE
PROMENADE FOR VISITORS AND CITIZENS TO
TAKE DAILY EXERCISE. JANE AND HER FAMILY
FREQUENTLY WALKED ALONG THIS SHORE
(1806-1809), SOMETIMES AS FAR AS CROSS HOUSE
QUAY, WHERE THE ITCHEN FERRY OPERATED.
ON 16 SEPTEMBER 1807 THE AUSTENS USED THE
FERRY TO VISIT NETLEY ABBEY. IN THE WINTER
THE MEADOWS FROZE AND JANE'S BROTHER
SKATED HERE.

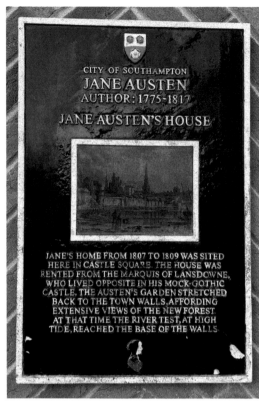

CITY OF SOUTHAMPTON
JANE AUSTEN
AUTHOR: 1775-1817
JANE AUSTEN'S HOUSE

JANE'S HOME FROM 1807 TO 1809 WAS SITED
HERE IN CASTLE SQUARE. THE HOUSE WAS
RENTED FROM THE MARQUIS OF LANSDOWNE,
WHO LIVED OPPOSITE IN HIS MOCK-GOTHIC
CASTLE. THE AUSTEN'S GARDEN STRETCHED
BACK TO THE TOWN WALLS, AFFORDING
EXTENSIVE VIEWS OF THE NEW FOREST.
AT THAT TIME THE RIVER TEST, AT HIGH
TIDE, REACHED THE BASE OF THE WALLS.

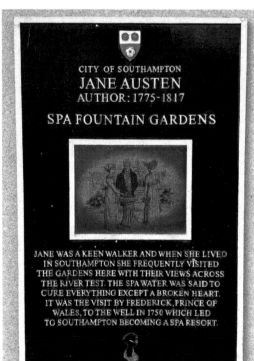

CITY OF SOUTHAMPTON
JANE AUSTEN
AUTHOR: 1775-1817

SPA FOUNTAIN GARDENS

JANE WAS A KEEN WALKER AND WHEN SHE LIVED
IN SOUTHAMPTON SHE FREQUENTLY VISITED
THE GARDENS HERE WITH THEIR VIEWS ACROSS
THE RIVER TEST. THE SPA WATER WAS SAID TO
CURE EVERYTHING EXCEPT A BROKEN HEART.
IT WAS THE VISIT BY FREDERICK, PRINCE OF
WALES, TO THE WELL IN 1750 WHICH LED
TO SOUTHAMPTON BECOMING A SPA RESORT.

Above left: Jane and family walked along The Platform.

Above right: Jane lived on the site of the Juniper Berry pub.

Left: The chalybeate water drinking fountain was where the lower level of the Westquay Waterstones is today.

19

The Victorian Era
(1837–1901)

Southampton saw a rapid increase in population from some 27,000 in 1841 to nearly 105,000 by the time of Queen Victoria's death in 1901. It was a period that saw the rapid expansion of the docks and development of trade, linked to the arrival of the railway in May 1840.

Expansion of the town saw a new wave in building construction such as the General Post Office at the lower end of the High Street (1892) and the imposing National Provincial Bank (1864) at Nos 129 and 130 High Street.

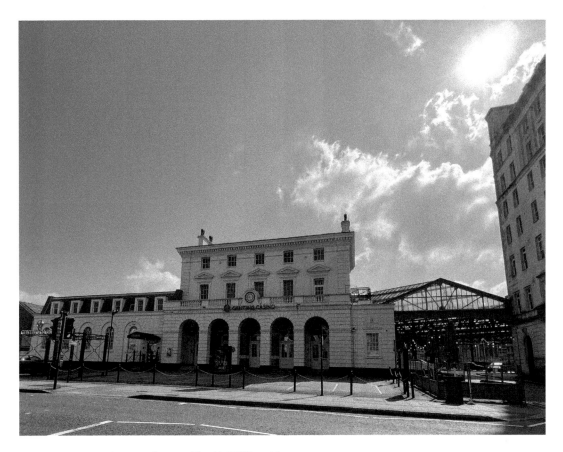

Terminus station was designed by Sir William Tite.

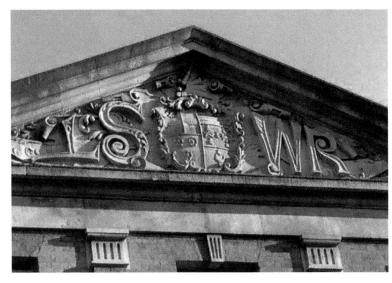

Left: The London & South Western Railway building in Canute Road.

Below left: The old post office in the High Street.

Below right: National Provincial Bank.

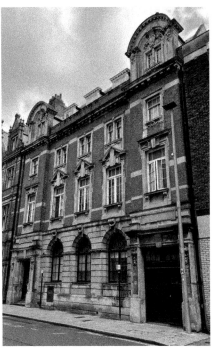

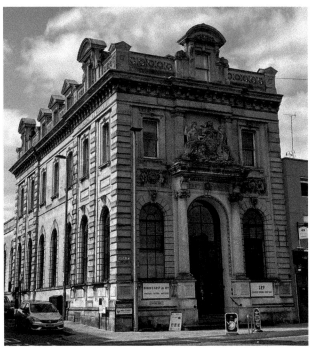

Living conditions for the working classes in the town remained grim, and there were cholera epidemics in 1848/49 and again in 1865. This latter outbreak saw the Board of Health appoint a new engineer, James Lemon, described as being 'about the right size to go up a sewer', who improved Southampton's sewage system.

The area of the town around Simnel Street was mainly slum houses in the nineteenth century. The population density of this part of Southampton was greater than that of Dickens's London.

In 1845 an Inspector of Prisons reported that God's House was totally inadequate. The council borrowed £14,000 to build a new one by 1855 in Ascupart Street, St Mary's. It was based on the model prison at Pentonville and designed for 120 prisoners in a strict regime of separate confinement. The responsibility for running the new prison rested with local magistrates and the council.

The census for 1861 lists a total of sixty-eight prisoners in the jail, ten of whom were women. Three of the ten women were prostitutes, one a girl of thirteen. Of the sixty-two prisoners in 1871 there were fourteen females, one of which was an eleven-month-old baby. The 1877 Prison Act transferred control of prisons to the Home Office. Southampton's prison was closed on 27 August, 1878.

Ellen Wren (1845–94), who often appeared before local magistrates, died in Simnel Street in her rented room. She choked on her own vomit after drinking gin. Her body was not discovered for some time. It is said that Ellen would take men to her room then attack them and steal their money. There was public outrage at the conditions some had to live in. As a result a programme of slum clearance was begun.

In 1833, Princess Victoria had stayed at The Star coaching inn prior to opening the original wooden Royal Pier. The current pier gatehouse dating from 1930 has a golden pineapple on top denoting welcome and friendship.

In April 1864 General Guiseppe Garibaldi (1807–82) visited Southampton. A procession through the streets drew large crowds. He stayed with Mayor George Brinton in East Park Terrace. Garibaldi is credited with Italian unification. He already had a biscuit named after him so Southampton named a pub in Crosshouse Road the Garibaldi Arms. It was destroyed by bombing in November 1940, killing fourteen people.

The South Western Hotel by the Terminus railway station was completed in 1872. Designed by architect John Norton, the hotel was linked to the station terminus by a canopy of glass and steel that is still in place today. The façade of the South Western Hotel on Canute Road is notable for its carved pediment and stone relief of Queen Victoria, who is surrounded by depictions of the Empire.

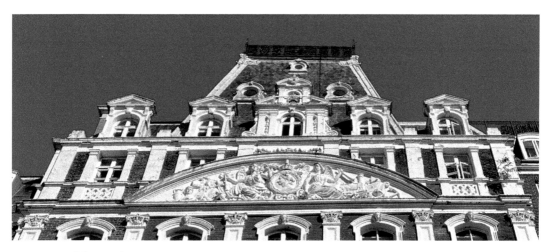

Front of the South Western Hotel.

With wars breaking out on the Continent and the need to defend the Empire, Southampton became a major military embarkation port, with troops departing for the Crimean War, the Zulu War and the South African War.

The foundation stone to the Royal Victoria Military Hospital at Netley was laid by Queen Victoria on 19 May 1856. Demolished in 1966, it is possible to climb the dome of the hospital's remaining chapel building and see magnificent views over Southampton Water.

In 1869, Mark Henry Blanchard was commissioned by Southampton's Mayor Sir Frederick Perkins to produce a terracotta statue of Prince Albert, the Prince Regent, to be installed in the Albert Infirmary at Bishops Waltham, which was then under construction. Blanchard's business was located on the site of Eleanor Coade's terracotta works at Lambeth.

The infirmary was not completed and, as five times mayor and the MP for Southampton, Perkins offered the statue to the town. In 1877, the borough surveyor James Lemon was instructed to place the statue at the east end of God's House Tower, the ground floor of which at that time was a mortuary.

The statue remained on the platform for about thirty years slowly deteriorating, often painted rather than cleaned and was eventually moved and put into storage.

In 1912 the council received a request from ratepayers for the statue to be restored but no action was taken. It is said that some Royal Engineers came across it during the First World War. On being informed it was the grandfather of the Kaiser they destroyed it.

The end of the Victorian era saw further developments such as the introduction of electric lighting and the electric tram system, which went through the central arch of the Bargate from 1900 until the 1930s.

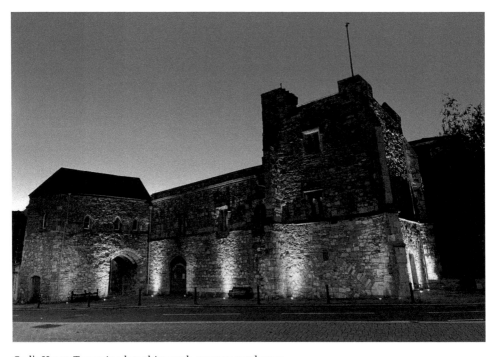

God's House Tower is a late thirteenth-century gatehouse.

Nineteenth-century Opium Trade

Southampton was a minor port in the 1830s, better known by yachtsmen than by merchants. So why did the East India Company make it its base for operations in China? Britain was desperate to increase trade with China and sell them our manufactured goods, which the Chinese rejected.

The East India Company (EIC) had surplus stocks of opium in their warehouses at Kolkata and decided to introduce it to the Chinese population. They engaged James Joseph Wolff (1797–1845), a ship's chandler, iron founder and manufacturer of ordnance, to secretly fit out four gunboats bound for Canton (Guangzhou) to enforce this trade. Southampton was chosen as a south coast port distant from EIC headquarters in London and suitable for such covert purposes.

Four iron paddle steamers were built by Lairds in Birkenhead (*Nemesis* and *Phlegethon*), and by Ditchburn & Mare in Deptford (*Pluto* and *Proserpine*). Nemesis was fitted with a large cannon in Portsmouth but the others were fitted out in Southampton.

Paddle steamers were needed to navigate the relatively shallow waters of the Guangzhou estuary, the only Chinese port permitted to trade with foreigners. Being flat-bottomed and not ideal for the open seas, they were equipped with sliding retractable keels which could be lowered in order to navigate rough passages such as the Cape of Good Hope.

The locally recruited crews were not told their destination. The four steamships all made a six-month voyage to Guangzhou. Once they arrived they were successful in attacking local shipping and promoting the opium trade. The first short-lived Opium War ended with a treaty in 1841. A reminder of this dubious incident in Southampton's past exists in the names of Amoy and Canton Streets in Bedford Place.

In June 1843 Woolf, who had a brass foundry in East Street, supplied twenty large cannons and explosives onto a ship called the *Tartar*. It was due to sail to Mexico to help their navy in a fight with the USA. However, there was a fire onboard at Chapel Wharf and the 20 tons of exploding gunpowder and shrapnel shells could be heard all over town. Woolf tried unsuccessfully to sink the *Tartar* with a gun on the platform.

In 1907, another HMS *Tartar* was the first Royal Navy ship to be built by the John Thornycroft yard at Woolston.

The Demon Drink

Today people today bemoan the fact that many of Southampton's pubs have closed. 150 years ago the opposite was the case. It was claimed that there were too many outlets selling alcohol and that many should close. Southampton was the third most drink-ridden town in England.

In 1878 the president of the St Mary's Church of England Temperance Society was the teetotal Basil Wilberforce, the rector of St Mary's. They published a Drink Map of Southampton showing the number of alcohol outlets in the town. Its purpose was to illustrate why Joseph Chamberlain MP could claim that Southampton was one of the most intemperate towns in England, with 1 person in every 120 having been charged with drunkenness. Chamberlain was advocating a system whereby a retail licence for the sale of spirits would be awarded to a trust with profits to be used for libraries, museums and parks. The 1878 map, unsurprisingly, proved very popular with the ships' crew when they were in town.

By the beginning of the twentieth century, the licensing magistrates were strict with the awarding of licences. Following the 1902 Licensing Act the number of licensed premises declined and convictions for drunkenness fell to 1 in 250 by 1908.

The local Licensing Authority took a hard line with licence renewals for notorious public houses. In 1912 the Bulls Head in French Street had a dubious reputation and was refused a licence. It was located in the present-day Medieval Merchants House.

The Ordnance Survey (OS) in Southampton since 1841

Formed in 1791, its original military purpose was to map Scotland following the suppression of the Jacobite rising of 1745. In 1841 the Ordnance Survey found their way to Southampton. A fire at the Tower of London had destroyed their London offices.

The original building, at the south end of the Avenue, was erected in the late eighteenth century at the onset of the French Revolutionary Wars as a cavalry barracks. The defeat of Napoleon at the Battle of Waterloo in 1815 made the barracks redundant. The building was converted in 1816 into a branch of the Royal Military Asylum looking after up to 400 orphan boys.

Between 1841 and 1867 new buildings were added. The buildings received some damage in the Blitz of 1940 and the work of the Survey was split between this site, Chessington in Surrey and the Crabwood House site at Maybush.

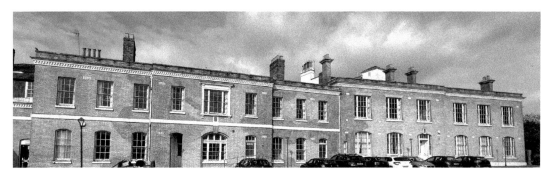

Above: Former Ordnance Survey building in London Road.

Right: Plaque outside the former OS building Barrack Block.

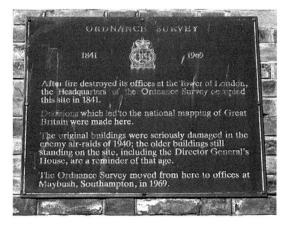

ORDNANCE SURVEY

1841 1969

After fire destroyed its offices at the Tower of London, the Headquarters of the Ordnance Survey occupied this site in 1841.

Decisions which led to the national mapping of Great Britain were made here.

The original buildings were seriously damaged in the enemy air-raids of 1940; the older buildings still standing on the site, including the Director General's House, are a reminder of that age.

The Ordnance Survey moved from here to offices at Maybush, Southampton, in 1969.

In 1969 a new permanent site was opened at Maybush and all operations were transferred there. The surviving buildings in London Road are from the mid-Victorian rebuilding. In 2010 the OS moved to new premises at Adanac Park by the M271.

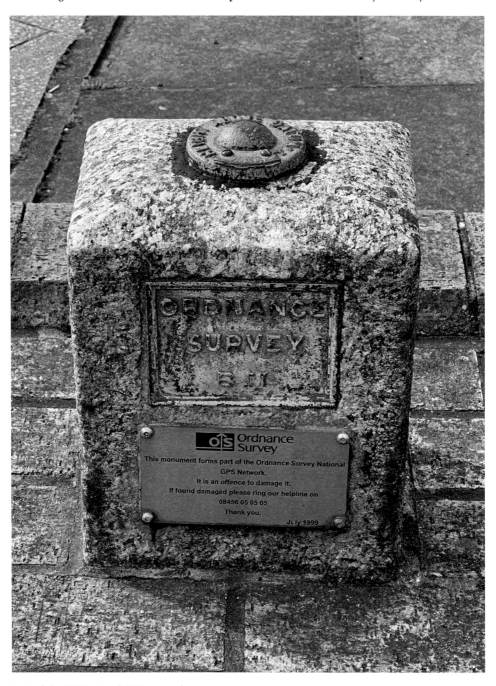

Part of the OS National GPS network.

23

Southampton FC – A Club Built on Faith since 1885

Why does our club have the nickname the Saints? Today's Southampton FC has its roots in a club formed in November 1885 by members of St Mary's Church of England Young Men's Association. Club president Basil Wilberforce was rector of St. Mary's from 1871 to 1894. William, his evangelical grandfather, had successfully led campaigns against slavery. Basil's father had been chaplain to Queen Victoria's husband Prince Albert.

Southampton St Mary's joined the Southern League in 1894, winning it from 1897 to 1899, and again in 1901, 1903 and 1904. They were losing FA Cup finalists in 1900 and 1902. Previously playing on the Common, the Antelope Ground in St Mary's Road and the County Cricket Ground in Northlands Road, Saints moved to their own new stadium called The Dell in 1898.

Founder members of the new Football League Third Division in 1920, they won promotion to the Second Division in 1922. Promotion to the First Division was narrowly missed in 1949.

Alf Charles was the first black Southampton FC player. The Trinidadian made just one first team appearance in January 1937. Terry Sealy was the second black player in 1977.

Relegation in 1953 sent the Saints back into the Third Division (South) until 1960 when they regained their Second Division status.

FirstDivision football came to The Dell in 1966, when manager Ted Bates' team were promoted as runners-up. Bates was replaced by his assistant Lawrie McMenemy in 1973.

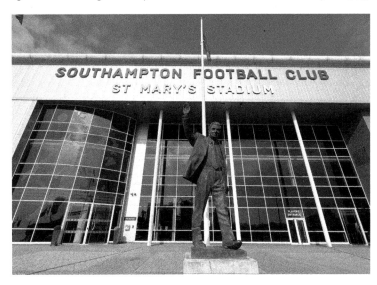

The Ted Bates statue in front of the Itchen Stand side of St Mary's Stadium.

Saints then became the first victims of the new three-down relegation system in 1974. Terry Paine left the club after eighteen years and over 800 league and cup games.

The most memorable day in Southampton FC's history came in 1976 when they were still a Second Division side. McMenemy led them to win the FA Cup for the first time with an against the odds 1-0 victory at Wembley over favourites Manchester United.

In 1978, Saints gained promotion back to First Division. Saints were beaten by Nottingham Forest in the 1979 League Cup final. In 1980 the signing of Kevin Keegan, twice European Footballer of the Year, stunned the football world.

In the 1983–84 season they were First Division runners-up to Liverpool. They also reached the FA Cup semi-finals, losing to Everton in extra time. They reached the FA Cup semi-finals again in 1986, losing to Liverpool.

In 1992, Southampton were founding members of the Premier League. One club man Matthew Le Tissier (b. 1968) scored 161 goals, including 47 out of 48 penalties.

The last league game at the Dell was played on 19 May 2001. The winning goal was from fan favourite Le Tissier to secure a 3-2 win over Arsenal. Saints then moved to the new 32,000-seat St Mary's Stadium.

Saints lost the 2003 FA Cup final to Arsenal. Southampton were relegated in the 2004/05 season. In 2009, Saints were relegated to League 1, the third level of English football. In financial administration, the club was bought out by Swiss-based, German-born entrepreneur Markus Liebherr. Sadly, he died in August 2010, by which time Saints were holders of the Johnstone's Paint Trophy.

Premier League football returned to St Mary's Stadium in August 2012. In 2015/16 under Ronald Koeman, they qualified for the UEFA Europa League for the second year running. They also reached the 2017 EFL Cup final, losing 3-2 to Manchester United.

In 2017 Gao Jisheng purchased a controlling interest in Southampton FC from Katharina Liebherr. In January 2022, his shareholding was purchased by Sport Republic.

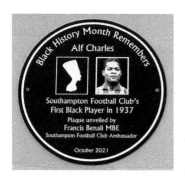

Left: Saints' first black footballer Alf Charles.

Below: St Mary's Stadium from the Northam footbridge.

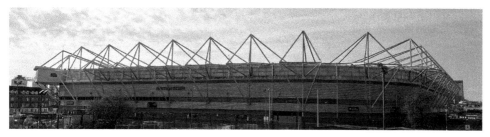

24

A Night to Remember

The 'unsinkable' *Titanic* ship made its maiden and final voyage from Southampton Docks. The largest moving object in the world left at midday on 10 April 1912.

The Slade brothers from Chantry Road in Chapel missed the departure as their way was blocked by a train going into the docks. They had boarded to attend muster at 8 a.m. then went to the Newcastle Hotel at the High Street end of East Street. They stopped at The Grapes in Oxford Street for one last drink. They are recorded as 'Deserted'.

After stops at Cherbourg and Queenstown, by 2.20 a.m. on 15th April *Titanic* had sunk just 2 hours and 40 minutes after it struck the iceberg at a speed of 20.5 knots. Of the 2,223 people aboard, the American investigation found 1,517 died and 706 survived. The dead included 832 passengers and 685 crew members. Of the 128 children, 67 were saved. Of the first-class passengers, mainly rich Americans, 62 per cent were saved. In second class it was 41 per cent and in third it was only 25 per cent. Only 23 per cent of the crew survived and nowhere was the impact felt more strongly than in Southampton where 550 families lost somebody. Of the 908 crew members, 724 were from a Southampton address.

For five days the names of survivors were posted up outside the Canute Road offices of the White Star Line, which in 1907 had moved from Liverpool.

My grandfather worked for White Star Lines on the *Olympic* but, luckily for me, was not chosen to be part of the crew for the *Titanic*'s maiden voyage.

Captain Edward Smith, who lived in Winn Road, perished along with over 500 crew members with a Southampton address. Many local women not only lost their men but also a breadwinner. In one school in Northam over half of the 240 children lost a father. One nine-year-old ended up in Shirley Warren workhouse.

The youngest survivor was Milvina Dean, who was born on 2 February 1912. She was also the longest living. She died at Woodlands, in May 2009, just outside Southampton on the edge of the New Forest.

The lookout who, without binoculars, first saw the iceberg was Fred Fleet. A survivor, in 1965 he took his own life at home in Norman Road, Fremantle, after his wife's death.

Mayor Henry Bowyer established the Titanic Relief Fund. Funds were distributed in small regular amounts by Miss Newman, riding around on her upright bike with her dalmatian dog running beside her. She performed the role of a social worker today and even found employment for one person as an apprentice at French & Sons Bootmakers. The business, dating from 1803, is still trading today in Bedford Place.

Mayor Bowyer died at the age of forty-eight in 1915 and is buried in the Old Cemetery on the Common. His cousin was experienced Trinity House pilot George Bowyer, who took control of *Titanic* as it left port, navigating it through the strong currents and sandbanks of the Solent. Harbour pilots are still used to this day.

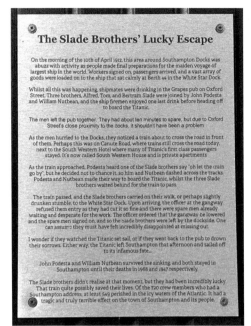

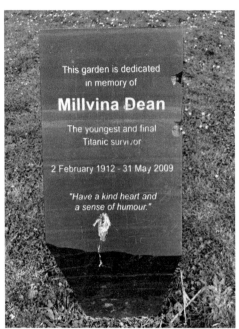

Above left: Slade Brothers plaque outside The Grapes pub in Oxford Street.

Above right: Millvina Dean plaque near SeaCity Museum.

The RMS *Carpathia* rescued just 705 passengers. The captain was Arthur Rostron (1869–1940), who is buried in West End. There is a Rostron Close at the bottom of Chalk Hill.

Southampton has a number of monuments including ones to the *Titanic*'s engineer officers and the musicians, all of whom died. The most poignant is a simple one to the crew in the ruins of Holy Rood paid for by those who were bereaved.

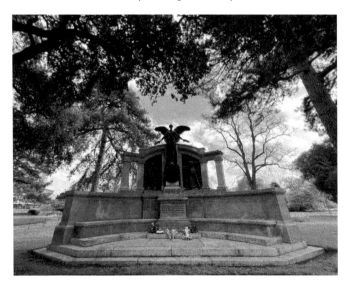

Monument to the *Titanic*'s engineers opposite the Cenotaph.

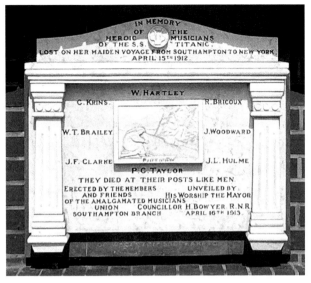

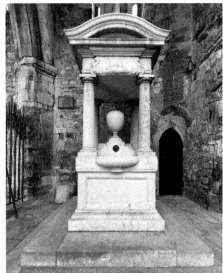

Above left: Plaque to the *Titanic*'s musicians.

Above right: Memorial inside Holy Rood.

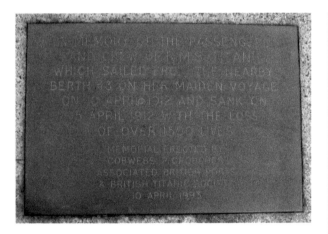

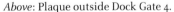

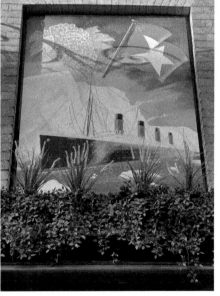

Above: Plaque outside Dock Gate 4.

Right: White Star Line mural on The Grapes pub.

At the Sea City Museum you can see first-hand items connected to the disaster and even hear the real voices of some survivors.

As a lasting reminder Cunard ships use the term White Star Service to describe the level of customer care expected of the company on their ships.

The company also has the White Star Academy, an in-house programme for new crew members. The White Star flag is raised on Cunard ships and on the *Nomadic* in Belfast, Northern Ireland, every 15th April in memory of the *Titanic* disaster.

25

Warhorses and Mutinies

During the First World War, Swaythling Remount Depot was the largest in England. Over 800,000 horses and mules were prepared for transportation to the Western Front. The port also saw over 8 million troops pass through.

The tank was very new and horses were far more effective in coping with the difficult terrain. One horse, Warrior, returned to become a police horse. After his death in 1935 he was buried near the first tee at Southampton Municipal Golf Course. More than 2,000 Sotonians died in the First World War. Their names are on the Cenotaph opened in 1920.

Following the First World War, there was social unrest. In January 1919 there was a wave of at least eighteen military mutinies including at Southampton docks, with troops refusing to embark to fight Russia communists. Around 5,000 disgruntled soldiers took over a customs shed in the docks.

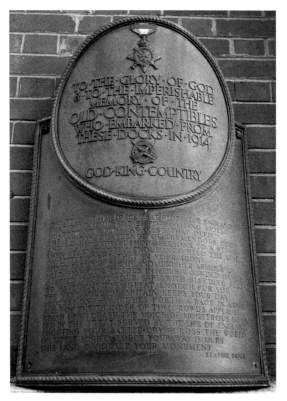

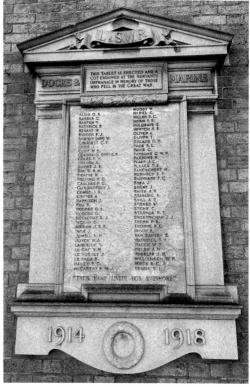

Above left: Plaque to the Old Contemptibles.

Above right: Plaque to the railway and docks employees.

General Hugh Trenchard made it clear that he would use lethal force. Trenchard had the mutineers surrounded by armed troops with their safety bolts in firing position and live ammunition. Fifty-three ringleaders were confined in a nearby troopship. Others had barricaded themselves in their billets. Hose pipes were used by Trenchard's riot squad. About 100 soaked men were then forced to stand in the January cold outside Trenchard's office.

In February, Trenchard was congratulated by Winston Churchill, then Minister for War and Air, for his 'masterly handling of the Southampton riots' and promoted him to Chief of the Air Staff.

In August 1919, up to 500 soldiers of the 27th Warwicks and the 25th Gloucesters also mutinied at Southampton. They believed that they were going to be sent from France to Russia where Winston Churchill's stated aim was 'to strangle at birth the Bolshevik State'. The soldiers posted notices on nearby railings saying 'We are being sent to Russia without being asked'.

During the evening Major-General Blackadder (no relation to the comedy character), commanding the troops in the Southampton district, arrived and a deputation of soldiers saw the general at the rest camp on Southampton Common but no resolution was reached. The next morning the mutineers would not submit voluntarily, so the Royal Sussex Regiment entered the enclosure on the Common and marched them off to waiting lorries.

26

The Gathering Storm in the 1930s

The Supermarine Company was founded in 1913 to develop flying boats. Spitfire designer R. J. Mitchell (1895–1937) joined as a racing seaplane designer in 1916 to help win the Schneider Trophy. The Supermarine S6B won the trophy outright in 1931. The prototype Spitfire first flew for eight minutes from Eastleigh Aerodrome, now part of Southampton International Airport, on 5 March 1936. A model is on the approach roundabout today. Sadly, Mitchell did not live to know the impact of his design.

By May 1940, the start of the Battle of Britain, every Spitfire scrambled to face the enemy had been built by Supermarine in the Southampton area. Following bombing in late September 1940 the Supermarine Works at Woolston and Itchen were permanently put out of action. The youngest to die was 'Shop Boy' Douglas Cruikshank at just fourteen. The bombing also destroyed the adjacent Itchen Ferry village. Plane production was dispersed from the Woolston and Itchen factories. Today, one slipway to the River Itchen remains. The design base was moved to Hursley Park, now part of the IBM site.

Many small locations were used in the area such as a small church hall in Shirley. Around 60 workers, mainly young women, sat at benches silver-soldering pipe fittings.

In 2018, a play performed locally, called *Shadow Factory*, told the story of the making of the plane that achieved legendary status in the Battle of Britain. Mitchell is buried at South Stoneham Cemetery and his house in Portswood has a blue plaque on it. Around sixty Spitfire planes survive worldwide.

The Civic Centre was designed by Ernest Berry Webber (1896–1963). It was his first major municipal design, built from 1929 to 1939. Pevsner described it as 'the most ambitious civic building erected in the provinces in the interwar year'.

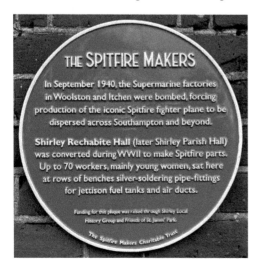

Plaque on Shirley Parish Hall.

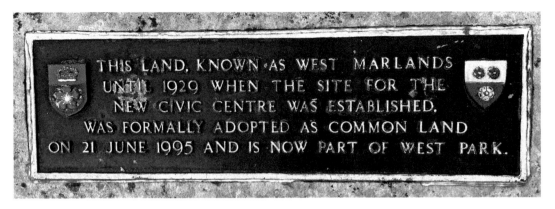

Plaque by the Civic Centre.

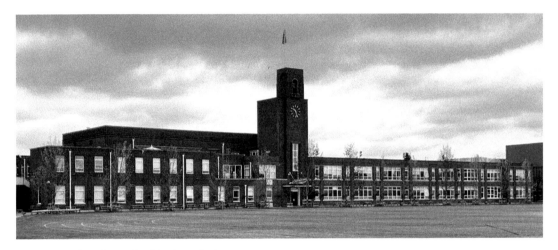

King Edward VI School built in the late 1930s.

Berry Webber also designed King Edward VI School in Hill Lane. Councillor and twice mayor Sidney Kimber (1873–1949) was the driving force behind this and other municipal projects such as Portswood Library and the Outdoor Sports Centre and Golf Course, completed in 1938.

Kimber's family owned the former brickworks which today is part of the campus of the University of Southampton. He was knighted in 1935. Kimber is buried at Highfield Church and Ernest Berry Webber designed the church's west porch in Kimber's honour.

On the evening of 5 July 1936 in a show of 'sabre rattling' the enormous silver-grey Hindenburg airship flew down the Solent towards Southampton Docks. The pride of the Nazis, complete with swastika emblems, was returning to Germany from New Jersey, USA. She travelled back down Southampton Water passing the RAF flying boat base at Calshot. Captain Lehmann denied accusations of spying. In 1937 Neville Shute wrote the book *Whatever Happened to the Corbetts*. It accurately predicted the bombing of Southampton.

On 23 May 1937, Southampton became a safe haven for 3,840 evacuee children, accompanied by Spanish Red Cross nurses and several priests. They came on the

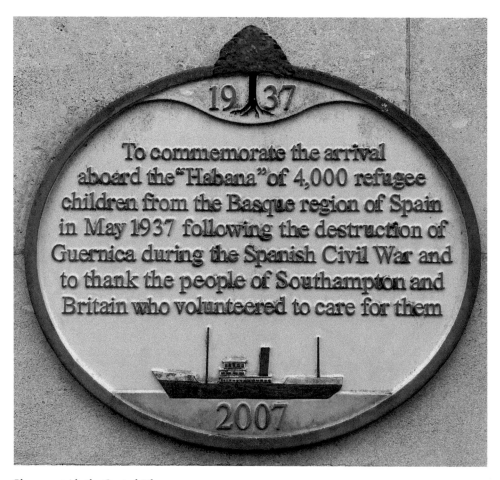

Plaque outside the Central Library.

SS *Habana* from the civil war torn Basque region of Spain. Initially, the British government did not want the children to come as intervention could be seen as taking sides.

After the town of Guernica was bombed by the German Luftwaffe in April 1937 the government allowed the children to come but only if taken in at the expense of private individuals. Around 1,000 people went to the Guildhall to pledge help and donate money. Initially the refugees were kept in 400 bell tents at Stoneham Farm. Daily activities included boxing organised by ex-heavyweight champion Joe Beckett (1892–1965), who lived in Shirley. The children were then dispersed to homes all over Britain.

INTERESTING EXTRA

About 400 Basque children settled permanently. One was the father of broadcaster Michael Portillo.

27

Got Any Gum, Chum?

The Civic Centre Art Gallery, only opened in April 1939, was bombed on 6 November 1940. George Brown, a town sergeant, was escorting a group of schoolchildren and their teachers around the gallery. When the air-raid warning sounded he took them down into the basement for safety. The bomb penetrated though and George along with fourteen of the children perished.

In 2006, Paul Tickner, himself a town sergeant, wrote a booklet chronicling the history of the town sergeants of Southampton over the last 700 years. The book was dedicated to George as the only one to lose his life in the execution of his duties.

From September to December 1940 a series of air raids by the German Air Force devastated Southampton. 2,631 high explosive and over 30,000 incendiary bombs were dropped on the town, killing 630 people and injuring 19,000. Over 3,500 buildings were destroyed and over 40,000 damaged. Overall, there were fifty-seven air raids on the town, which was easy to reach by German forces in occupied northern France. Many children were evacuated to safer nearby places.

A persistent urban myth is that Luftwaffe crews were ordered not to bomb St Michael's Church as the tall spire was needed for the planes to navigate by. The Second World War air raids were far more indiscriminate than today's precision bombing. Nearby Holyrood Church also had a spire but was destroyed. Air raids were often carried out at night during a 'blackout' and the crew would have relied on eyesight.

The areas around the docks and the Spitfire factory in Woolston suffered badly from bombing, especially in late 1940.

The British Expeditionary Force sailed from Southampton to Cherbourg on 9 September 1939. Seven months later, they returned, many rescued by the 'Dunkirk Little Ships'. Troops left the town for postings all over the world. The wounded, refugees and German prisoners of war came in on returning ships.

Early on Southampton was identified as a pivotal port for the launch of an invasion of Europe. The South Western Hotel was requisitioned as HMS *Shrapnel* and became the headquarters for Combined Operations Military Movement Control. Churchill and Eisenhower met here on at least one occasion. The room is still preserved as it was.

The invasion plans required the construction of two artificial harbours to be towed to Normandy immediately after the landings to facilitate the unloading of supply ships. Secret construction of the codenamed 'Mulberry Harbours' began in the dry docks in spring 1943, with component parts built along the south coast.

A pipeline under the ocean (PLUTO) was made at the Pirelli factory in Southampton. It ran from the Isle of Wight to Cherbourg to supply fuel for the Allied vehicles.

In the summer of 1943, the US Army Transportation Corps took over the docks and it was designated the US Army 14th Major Port. Their first task was *Operation Bolero* to

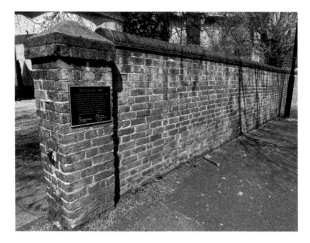

The D-Day Wall has names carved by US troops.

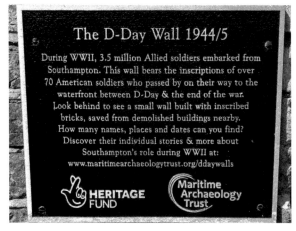

Plaque about the D-Day Wall.

discharge the lend-lease cargoes from America. The United States supplied the UK and other Allies with food, oil, vehicles, locomotives, aircraft and warships.

The 14th Port was then responsible for the embarkation of troops and equipment destined for Normandy from D-Day onwards. They received war casualties and German prisoners, the repair and salvage of vessels, and finally organised the repatriation of troops, equipment and war brides to America.

At its peak in November 1944, US Port military personnel numbered 6,641 with around 700 civilian personnel. The whole of Southampton effectively became a military camp with the surrounding area as far as Romsey and Winchester identified as Area C.

Camps for British and American soldiers were in the grounds of the big local houses at Chilworth, Broadlands and Hursley. Canadians were camped at Bassett Wood, Bassett Green and Stoneham Golf Course. Adanac is Canada backwards and Adanac Park is the current site of the Ordnance Survey.

Between D-Day 6 June 1944 and the end of the Second World War, 3.5 million mainly American and Canadian troops passed through Southampton and onto France.

The 399th Truck Company needed 100 buses and trucks to bring the 2,000 stevedores into the docks every day.

At this time, the US Army had segregation – black and white troops were not allowed to mix. White US officers were billeted in the Polygon Hotel and in private houses in Highfield and Bassett. Troops were billeted at many of the schools following their evacuation, including Ascupart Road, King Edward's, Swaythling Junior and Taunton's schools and at the Blighmont Barracks at Millbrook.

INTERESTING EXTRA
Blighmont House was built in the early 1800s by Admiral Richard Bligh for his son, George. He fought on Nelson's flagship HMS *Victory* at the 1805 Battle of Trafalgar and was a cousin of William Bligh of Mutiny on the Bounty fame.

The US Army control centre was in the Civic Centre, while the US Naval Advance Amphibious base operated from the Star Hotel. The US 28th and 46th Field Hospitals were set up to receive the most seriously wounded soldiers returning after D-Day. The Royal Victoria Hospital at Netley was taken over by the Americans.

At the Red Cross clubs, men could access laundry services, barbers and enjoy recreational activities, sports, movies and four dances a week. American football was played at the Dell. American troops entertained children and gave them chocolate, comics, rides in their Jeeps and even Christmas parties.

Some of the young women of Southampton enjoyed being treated to a pair of nylons and invited to dances. The former Gaiety cinema in the High Street was the main cinema used for dates by American servicemen. Locals said that the US troops were 'Overpaid, oversexed and over here'. The children's cries of 'Got any gum chum' were often met by the retort 'Got a sister mister?'

The Far East Prisoners of War (FEPOW) memorial in Town Quay Park remembers the troops brought home to Southampton by merchant navy ships.

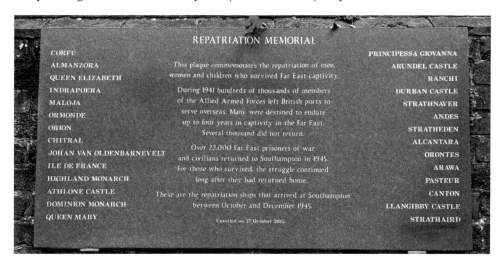

Far East Prisoner of War (FEPOW) memorial in Town Quay Park.

28

Time Capsules of History

In many ways churches are time capsules of history. Their history and contents are a valuable resource to understand the past.

The east window at St Michael's Church shows the five churches that stood within the medieval walls of Southampton. Only St Michael's, from 1070, remains an active church. It has a black Tournai marble font from 1170, one of only seven known ones existing, of which four are in Hampshire.

There are two brass eagle lecterns. The larger, dating from the late 1300s, is one of the finest in the country. It was rescued from Holy Rood when it was bombed in 1940. The church had to be reconsecrated after the 1338 French raid. Many had fled here for sanctuary but were slain inside. The most famous tomb is to Richard Lyster (1480–1554). He was Lord Chief Justice during the reign of Henry VIII.

St Michael's spire was added in the 1400s and reconstructed in 1732. In 1878, to make it a better landmark for shipping, a further 9 feet were added making it 165 feet. Town mayors were sworn in at St Michael's until 1835.

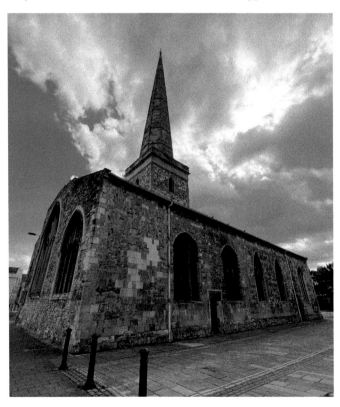

St Michael's Church.

St John the Baptist Church, in French Street, was demolished in 1708. The twelfth-century St Lawrence's was rebuilt in 1842 and demolished by 1925. The Standing Order pub is on the site today and incorporates part of the north church wall.

Holy Rood dates from 1320 but has Anglo-Saxon roots. The Holy Rood is thought to be the cross on which Jesus died. The church was largely destroyed in a November 1940 bombing raid.

Once, people would gather in front of it to celebrate the arrival of the New Year. The 'Sailor's Church', where they once prayed before a journey, is now preserved as a Merchant Navy memorial. In front of the church is a small brass cross in the pavement marking a lucky escape. In 1862, Lord Palmerston, the Prime Minister, was passing on his way to open the nearby Hartley Institution, a forerunner of the University of Southampton. People were watching from the tower and a stone ball fell off, missing Palmerston.

All Saints was built in 1795 on the site of an earlier church. Damaged in the Southampton Blitz of 1940, it was never rebuilt. Jane Austen worshipped in it during her time here. The East Street car park is built over its graveyard.

Outside the Old Town, St Mary's has a link back to a AD 694 visit of St Birinus. The present church, rebuilt after bombing, is the sixth on the site. The 'Bells of St Mary's' song was popularised by the 1940 film starring Bing Crosby. It was written by Furber and Adams, who had heard St Mary's bells on an earlier visit to Southampton.

Press gangs operated in Southampton and were paid well. In 1757, Guernseyman John de la Mere threw himself from the town walls rather than be pressed into the service of the Navy. He was buried in St Mary's churchyard.

Across the River Itchen, St Mary's Extra, known as Pear Tree Church, dates from 1620. It was the first new Anglican church in England to be built following the Reformation of the sixteenth century.

St Julien's Chapel in Winkle Street is named after the patron saint of pilgrims. It was originally built as part of a hospice, Maison Dieu, in 1196 by the wealthy Gervais Le Riche. It was for the use of pilgrims on their way from France to visit the tomb of Thomas à Becket at Canterbury.

In 1445 the fifteen-year-old Princess Margaret of Anjou arrived in Southampton and rested at St Julien's Chapel before going 12 miles to Titchfield to marry Henry VI.

Belgian Walloons and French Huguenots were given permission by Elizabeth I to use St Julien's for services in French as long as the English prayer book was followed. The church has a bricked-up lepers' window.

Netley Abbey, to the east of Southampton, was constructed in the mid-thirteenth century and was home for fifteen Cistercian monks. When monasteries across Britain were dissolved by King Henry VIII, Netley was one of the first to go in 1536.

The king granted it to Sir William Paulet, treasurer of the royal household, as a reward for loyal service. Eventually abandoned, the neglected site became overgrown with trees and ivy, before it became celebrated as 'the romantic ruin'.

Authors and artists, including Jane Austen, would visit Netley Abbey for inspiration.

In the Victorian age, new churches were constructed, meeting the needs of the increasing suburban population. They included Christ Church, Freemantle (1865/66) and

Holy Trinity Millbrook (1874) to the west; St Denys' (1868) and Christ Church, Highfield (1847), in the north; and Holy Saviour, Bitterne (1852) and Peartree Congregational Church (1838) to the east.

A Quaker cemetery has been located since the 1660s where Brighton Road joins the Avenue.

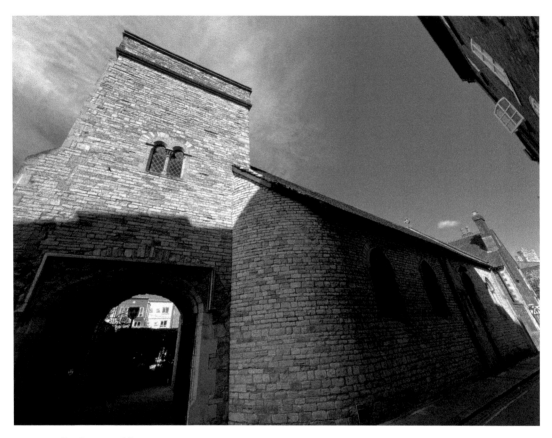

St Julien's in Winkle Street.

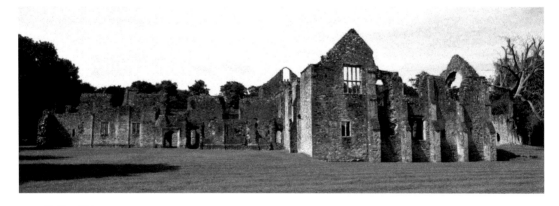

Netley Abbey.

A City Rising by the Sea

After the Second World War bomb damage the most pressing issue was housing. One answer was for the council to build temporary prefabs. Although basic, they were well liked by residents who were often reluctant to leave many years later.

Post-war rebuilding continued with the east side of Above Bar Street completed in 1954. The steel frames were clad with Portland stone. Tyrrell & Green department store was reopened in 1956. Pevsner said that 'few department stores, and no others in Southampton, have reached this standard'. The final Above Bar Street store to be rebuilt was Plummers in 1965. The building is currently used by the University of Southampton.

INTERESTING EXTRA
The abbreviations of Soton and Sotonian were coined by journalists at the *Daily Echo*, who found Southampton and Southamptonian too long to fit easily into the newspaper's headlines.

A sign of Southampton's post-war rebirth was the awarding of city status. Back in 1918, Mayor Kimber had raised this possibility. In 1964, Mayor Pugh read a letter out in the Mayor's Parlour which said 'Her Majesty the Queen has been graciously pleased to raise the town and county of the town of Southampton to the title and dignity of a city'.

Some Notable Sotonians

Dame Claramunda (early 1200s)
There is a tiled picture of her on Queen's House in the Holyrood estate.

Richard Cockle Lucas (1800–83)
The sculptor and artist lived in Chilworth and is best known for his 1861 statue of Isaac Watts in West Park. In 1909 a museum in Berlin bought one of his paintings, incorrectly thinking it was by Leonardo da Vinci.

Frederick Lee Bridell (1830–63)
The artist was exhibited at the Royal Academy when only twenty-one. His *The Temple of Love* was compared to Turner. The *Colosseum in Rome by Moonlight* is his best-known work.

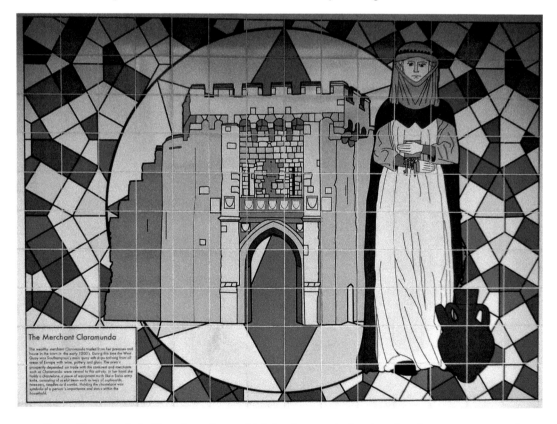

Dame Claramunda holds a chantelane, which has keys on it showing that she was a woman of status.

William Burrough Hill (1845–1941)

An art collector, he called his home in Regents Park Bridell Lodge,m having bought his *Colosseum in Rome* painting in 1929. In the 1890s he employed William Marshall Cooper to paint sixty-five watercolours of the Old Town area before slum clearance.

Kate Sclater (1863–1940)

Southampton born Kate became a leader of the 1888 Match Girls Strike at the Bryant and May factory in Bow, East London. George Bernard Shaw is said to have based his Eliza Doollittle character in *Pygmalion* on Kate.

Lucia Foster Welch (1864–1940)

A suffragette who was the first female to become a councillor in 1918. As the first female mayor in 1928 she greeted aviator Amelia Earhart after her transatlantic flight. In 2022, Jacqui Rayment became Southampton's 800th mayor, the 31st female and the first one to be a lord mayor.

Miss Ethel Newman (1876–1940)

Lived all her life in Hawthorn Cottage on the Common. The 'Lady on the Bike' administered the Titanic Relief Fund money to bereaved dependents.

Edwin Moon (1886–1920)

The fourteenth-century Woolhouse is now the Dancing Man Brewery. In the early 1900s it was run by a family firm as the Moonbeam Engineering Company. There Edwin built a monoplane, *Moonbeam II*, which became the first aeroplane to fly from what became Southampton Airport.

In 1909, Edwin was one of the first people locally to get fined for speeding in a motor car. He died in a flying boat accident and is buried at Southampton Old Cemetery with the propeller on the grave.

Elsie Sandell (1891–1974)

A writer of local history books and articles. Sandell Court in Bassett is named in her honour.

Ivor Montagu (1905–85)

The first president of the Saints Supporters club. His father was Lord Swaythling and he grew up in Townhill Park House, now the independent Gregg School. He went on to become Alfred Hitchcock's co-producer on films such as *The Thirty Nine Steps* (1930). He also spied for Russia. His brother Ewen Montagu (1901–1985) worked in British naval intelligence devising *Operation Mincemeat*. *The Man That Never Was* film (1956) told this true wartime story. It duped the German forces into thinking there would be a major Allied invasion of Greece when it was actually Sicily.

Sir Christopher Cockerell (1910–99)

In 1959 a prototype hovercraft he designed made its first journey on Southampton Water. He lived for many years in Hythe.

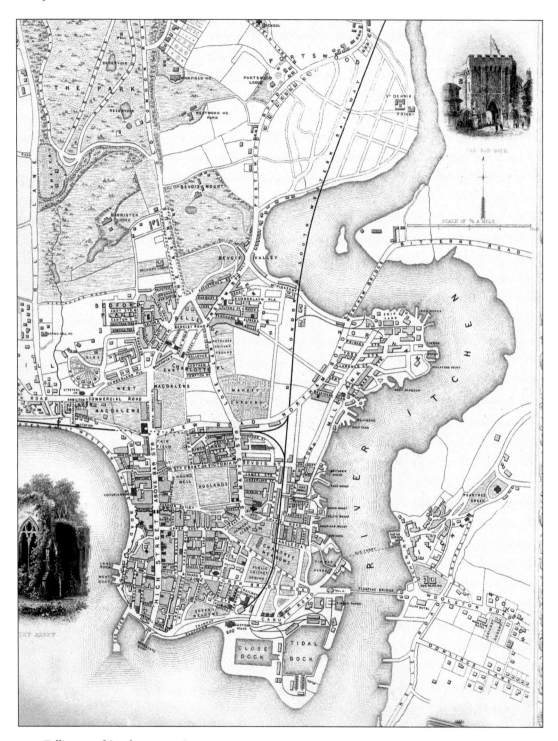

Tallis map of Southampton, 1851.

Sir Edward Penley Abraham (1913–99)
Born in South View Road, Shirley, he was instrumental in the development of the antibiotics penicillin and cephalosporin.

N. J. Crisp (1923–2005)
A prolific scriptwriter, his credits included *Dixon of Dock Green, Dt. Finlay's Casebook, The Expert, Colditz* and *Secret Army*. He lived in Abbotts Way, Portswood.

Benny Hill (1924–92)
The comedian was born in Bernard Street and had a successful film and TV career.

Don Shinn (1945–2023)
Keyboard wizard Don played with artists including Rod Stewart, Dusty Springfield and Engelbert Humperdinck. Keith Emerson of Emerson, Lake and Palmer acknowledged he was influenced by Don's playing style.

Craig David (1981–present)
Growing up on the inner-city Holyrood estate, Craig has sold over 15 million records.

INTERESTING EXTRA
Roger Moore's stuntman in some James Bond films, Sam Costa, used to run the Joiners Arms in the early 1980s.

A Southampton Timeline

c. 1500 BC	England's oldest bridge at Testwood Lakes by the River Test.
c. 70	Roman town called Clausentum at Bitterne Manor.
c. 407	Romans leave Britain.
Mid-sixth century	King Ine builds Hamwih, a Saxon town in the St Mary's area.
Ninth and tenth centuries	Viking raids.
c. 950	River Itchen silts up and the town relocates to the west.
1070	Normans start building of St Michael's Church.
1086	The town becomes a royal borough.
1124	St Denys' Priory is founded by Henry I.
c. 1180	The Bargate is built.
1189	Foundation of Maison Dieu (God's House) Hospice.
1197	Approximate date that St Julien's Church is established.
1200	Approximate date that the Long House was built.
1217	First mayor mentioned.
1228	The Common is bought for the citizens.
1233	Approximate date that the Franciscan Friary is founded.
1236	Jews expelled.
1239	Netley Abbey is founded near the town.
1299	Old Bowling Green is in use.
Late thirteenth century	God's House Tower built as a gatehouse into the Old Town.
1300	Southampton's population is approximately 5,000.
1319	Venetian state fleet visits Southampton.
1320	Holyrood Church built.
1332	Wool House built.
1338	The town is attacked by French and Genoese pirates.
1346	Edward III and his son the Black Prince sail for the Battle of Crecy.

1348	The Black Death strikes, killing a quarter of the population.
1415	In August the ringleaders of the Southampton Plot to depose Henry V are executed at Bargate.
1445	The charter of incorporation is given to the town by Henry VI.
1491	Tudor House and Garden is built.
1553	King Edward VI school founded.
1554	Philip of Spain visits the town on way to marry Mary Tudor.
1567	French and Belgian Protestants settled and were granted St Julien's Chapel by Elizabeth I.
1596	Population is 4,200.
1600	Described as a 'decayed port'.
1618	Southampton Castle is in ruins and sold.
1620	Departure of the *Mayflower* and *Speedwell* for America on 15 August.
1665	Plague kills 1,700.
1669	King Charles II visits.
1750	Prince Frederick swims here and the spa town era starts.
1760	Taunton's School founded.
1761	Assembly Rooms were built.
1766	Theatre Royal is built in French Street.
1778	Southampton gets its first bank.
1795	All Saints Church is built.
1798	Thorners Charity was built.
1799	First Northam Bridge.
1800	Population around 8,000.
1802	Salisbury and Southampton Canal.
1831	Southampton's population is 19,324.
1833	Royal Pier, opened by the Duchess of Kent and Princess (later Queen) Victoria, opens. It was closed in 1979 and is now derelict.
1836	Woolston Floating Bridge.
1837	Southampton Dock Company is incorporated.

1838	Royal South Hants Hospital, founded with help from local Masons.
1839	The Terminus railway station opens.
1840	Railway from Nine Elms, London, is completed.
1841	The Ordnance Survey arrives. Southampton's population is 27,744.
1842	The first dock opens.
1846	Southampton Old Cemetery on the Common.
1847	The Riding School at Carlton Place is completed.
1848	Cholera kills 151 people.
1855	Southampton School of Art and the prison on Ascupart Street are established.
1856	Royal Victoria Military Hospital at Netley opens.
1861	Red Funnel ferries start operating services to the Isle of Wight.
1862	Hartley Institute is founded in the High Street, a forerunner of the University of Southampton.
1866	Cholera outbreak.
1874	Hythe Pier is built and Hythe and Southampton Ferry Company is formed. A ferry service starts in 1880 after the pier is completed.
1875	The Isaac Watts Memorial Hall is built. The Royal Southampton Yacht Club is chartered.
1876	Above Bar Church founded.
1879	Southampton Tramways Company begins operating.
1885	St Mary's Young Men's Association Football Club and the Hampshire Field Club are established.
1889	Southampton Free Public Library established.
1895	Fremantle, Millbrook and Shirley become part of Southampton. Southampton West, now Southampton Central, railway station opens.
1898	The Dell football stadium opens.
1900	General Hospital founded as the Southampton Union Infirmary.
1901	Southampton's population is 104,824.
1902	Warsash Maritime School founded, with its current campus in St Mary's opening in 2017.

1907	White Star Line relocates to Southampton from Liverpool.
1908	Southampton Water is a sailing and motor boating venues for the Summer Olympics.
1912	On 10 April, the *Titanic* departed Southampton on her maiden and final voyage. In July Tudor House Museum opens.
1913	*Mayflower* memorial erected.
1914	On 22 April, the Titanic Engineers' Memorial is unveiled in East Park. From August, Southampton's docks are used to take soldiers, supplies and horses to France following the outbreak of war.
1919	Cunard Line relocates to Southampton from Liverpool.
1920	Bassett, Bitterne, Itchen and Swaythling became part of Southampton.
1920	Cenotaph memorial unveiled in Watts Park.
1928	The Empire Theatre opens, becomes the Gaumont in 1950 and since 1987 has been known as the Mayflower.
1929	Building works start for the Civic Centre.
1932	First phase of Civic Centre opened by Duke of York, later King George VI.
1932	Southampton Municipal Airport established.
1933	King George V opens New Western Docks and the Graving Dock, which is named after him.
1937	Guildhall opens.
1938	Outdoor Sports Centre and Municipal Golf Course opens.
1939	Art Gallery and Library opens.
1940	Extensive bombing raids in November and December.
1949	The last tram runs on New Year's Eve.
1952	The University of Southampton receives its charter.
1954	Northam Bridge is rebuilt using concrete.
1955	Bird's Eye fish fingers tested on the Southampton public.
1961	The Museum of Archaeology opens in God's House Tower.
1964	The city of Southampton was created.
1966	Southampton Maritime Museum opens in the Wool House.

1968	First Southampton Boat Show.
1969	Southampton Technical College is established.
1976	Southampton's hottest June day ever as it reaches 35.6°C (96.1°F).
1977	The Woolston Floating Bridge stops operating to be replaced by the Itchen Toll Bridge.
1984	Solent Sky aviation museum opens.
1985	Medieval Merchants House is restored.
1986	The UK's first geothermal power scheme opens. Its users include the Civic Centre, Solent University and the Royal South Hants Hospital.
1986	The Ocean Village area is redeveloped. The five-star Harbour Hotel is not completed until 2017.
1989	Bargate Shopping Centre opens.
1990	The Marlands Shopping Centre opens.
1995	The M3 motorway from London is completed.
1996	The Oceanography Centre opens.
2000	Westquay shopping centre opens on 28 September.
2005	Southampton Solent University is created.
2009	Carnival House office building opens reflecting the growth in the cruise ship business.
2012	On 10 April Southampton commemorates the 100th anniversary of the sinking of *Titanic*. The SeaCity Museum opens.
2013	Bargate Shopping Centre closes, and its demolition begins in November 2017.
2016	Westquay Watermark opens.
2021	Southampton Airport is named as the best in the UK and the third best globally for sustainability performance.
2021	Southampton's population is 261,729.
2022	Southampton is one of the four cities to be shortlisted to be the City of Culture in 2025 but loses to Bradford.
2023	On 18 February, all red First Bus services discontinued, ending a local link that went back to the horse-drawn trams of 1879.